# DON'T BEND WALLA WALLA

## A Case Study in Corruption

### by Daniel N. Clark

Walla Walla, Washington
2014

# Contents

# Don't Bend Walla Walla
## A Case Study in Corruption

## 1. A Proposal & The Community's Response

The concerns of the Walla Walla 2020 citizens group about sprawling development were well-known in our community by 2003, fifteen years after its founding. Late that year, as coordinator of the group I received a call from City of Walla Walla planning director Robert Horn wondering what our group would think of a proposal for a new golf course and upscale housing project to be located on 380 acres of prime farmland across a state highway from the Walla Walla airport and extending towards the beloved Blue Mountains. The proponent, Pennbrook Homes of Bend, Oregon, was expressing an interest in annexing this property into the city. Bend at that time was one of the fastest growing areas in the country and was a symbol of runaway development.

Knowing that the last thing most people in Walla Walla wanted was development creep toward the beautiful Blues, I told Bob that while I couldn't speak for Walla Walla 2020 since we hadn't considered the project, I thought the group might consider going along with the proposal if the developers were to agree to buy conservation easements on the land directly east of the property to prevent further creep toward the mountains, which they might themselves be contemplating.

Pennbrook apparently wasn't interested in that approach, and proceeded to implement its project by filing an application to expand our community's Urban Growth Area to include the proposed site through an amendment to the Urban Area Comprehensive Plan.

The Port of Walla Walla, owner of the Walla Walla Regional Airport, initially opposed the project, notifying the city of its concerns about "allowing housing and other non-compatible land uses to surround the airport." The Port specifically cited the problem of placing housing in the vicinity of two runways which lead directly over the project site. It raised additional concerns regarding the inability to predict future needs and use of the airport, including level of use by private, commercial, and military aircraft, citing in particular the ability of the federal government to take over the airport for military use under prior agreements. The Port's existing master plan discouraged new housing development in the vicinity of the airport, declaring that "In recent years, a new residential development area was permitted northeast of the airport, which could cause potential land use conflicts in the future. Additional residential development located in the vicinity of the airport should be discouraged."

Despite that, in March 2004, the Port and Pennbrook began discussions about the project, including how the Port might supply water to the development as a revenue source to the Port rather than connecting the project to the city's water system. In the course of those discussions the Port advised the developer against annexing to the City.

In August 2004, notwithstanding its earlier protests, the Port drafted, submitted, and began lobbying the County and City to change existing planning and water conservation policies by adopting new policies specifically crafted for Pennbrook's Illahee project, including the elimination of prohibitions against housing encroachment in the vicinity of the airport, as well as authorization for the Port to become a water supplier for nearby residential development in place of the existing requirement that the City of Walla Walla be the sole supplier for new water connections in the Urban Area.

Walla Walla 2020 and another local group, Citizens for Good Governance, opposed these changes, and were joined by other concerned citizens, one of whom created a popular bumper sticker reading "Don't Bend Walla Walla."

Besides pointing out that the proposed changes violated the county's established procedural deadlines and other planning rules, Walla Walla 2020 stated its initial protest in this way:

> Regarding the merits of the proposed policy amendments and map amendments relating to the Pennbrook development, lands with productive soils and viability for agriculture should be protected from housing and commercial development which forever remove it from productivity. This land has extremely high productivity, and based on soils, rainfall, and production history is some of the most fertile and productive in Walla Walla county, even without irrigation. Sacrificing it to high-end commercial development with increased water use at a time of diminishing supplies, plus the inexorable pressure on prime farmland adjoining the site, violates multiple policies of our comprehensive plan and will contribute to inefficient and unsightly sprawl. Any need for growth should be accommodated through higher-density development within walking distance of urban services rather than expansion of the urban area into prime farmland. Such development creates problems for transportation, as well as for efficient delivery of other services.

In spite of various objections, on October 31, 2005, the Walla Walla County Commissioners unanimously approved a variety of changes to the Walla Walla Urban Area Comprehensive Plan sought by Pennbrook and the Port, including putting the project site into the UGA and adding an Urban Planned Communities (UPC) chapter to the county zoning code. Though Citizens for Good Governance filed an appeal of those actions to the state's Growth Management Hearings Board for Eastern Washington, following the Port's formal intervention in the appeal proceeding in order to protect its new water utility venture, the appeal was rejected.

On November 2, 2005, the Walla Walla City Council also voted 6-1 to allow the utility agreements between the Port and Pennbrook to proceed. The dissenting member of the council gave the following explanation for her refusal to agree:

> Long before this council or the general public had any notion of its existence, the Pennbrook development had been embraced by the County, which had already decided that the project would be built no matter what. At that time the proposed development wasn't consistent with the County's own Comprehensive Plan, so the County hired a consultant to be on its planning staff for as long as it took—not to do planning in the public interest but to determine what amendments had to be made to the Comprehensive Plan to allow the Pennbrook development to go forth. The consultant's salary is paid by Pennbrook.

Six members of the council want to see the project proceed and many months ago gave direction to our staff to help make that happen. Recently, the Council has publicly expressed concern that the Port rather than the City will be the water purveyor for the development, but matters were set in motion by the earlier Council direction and at this point it seems clear that the Port will provide water to Pennbrook.

I'll be voting No for the following reasons:

We often speak of a limited water supply. As recently as 12 years ago there was discussion about the fact that the water level in City wells and others throughout our valley had been falling at a rate of three to five feet per year for 50 years. At the levels of population and industrial and agricultural water usage of those years, we were pulling water out of our aquifers faster than they were being naturally recharged, and we were heading toward a crisis.

Water is an essential resource that needs to be managed to benefit the whole community. Limits are real and likely to become more so with global warming and population growth.

The water advisory committee created by the Council at that time introduced the idea of artificial recharge of the aquifers. That program has stabilized and raised water levels in some City wells.

The Port's old and newly-acquired wells are drilled into the same limited aquifer as the City's wells which have been retrofitted to recharge that aquifer. The Port's well will be able to supply cheap water to Pennbrook only because of the City's recharge of the aquifer, for which service the Port does not pay.

With that background, I think that it is irresponsible to create a new purveyor for residential development instead of working to create a unified water management and delivery plan to assure water availability at fair rates for those who live here. We should not be further fragmenting water systems in the Valley.

If the City had provided water to Pennbrook, it would have been at the same rate we charge to all our water customers. Our rates cover treatment and delivery of water, including the aquifer recharge program, and some regular maintenance. Extraordinary capital costs require bonds, grants, or low-interest loans. Delivering safe water to our customers is not a profit-making venture for the City.

The Port and Pennbrook, however, will be selling water as a revenue source. Because the City's aquifer recharge program supports the capacity of the Port's wells, the Port and Pennbrook will have cheap water, subsidized in their business venture by the City's water customers who are paying their fair share of the costs.

Finally, I believe this arrangement corrupts the market system which we rely on to set values in the economy. Although our water supply is limited, the Port and Pennbrook do not have any incentive to conserve. Because it's subsidized, their water is relatively cheap, and the more they sell, the greater their revenue.

Further, just like the Pennbrook folks, local developers must also build infrastructure—streets, sidewalks, and utility connections. But they do not receive, as Pennbrook will, cheap water as a revenue source to offset those construction costs. Government should not subsidize Pennbrook to give them an advantage over local developers.

I expect county government, the port district, and city government to work for the public interest, not for one specially-privileged developer.

Having both city and county approval, Pennbrook filed a development application in December, 2005 for an Urban Planned Community of 365 single-family homes, a nine-hole golf course, hotel, restaurant, and related commercial facilities on 358 acres south and east of Highway 12, west of Harbert Road, and just north of the City's water treatment plant.

Robert Rittenhouse ,Walla Walla 2020 president and a chemistry professor at Walla Walla College, explained 2020's objections further in a May 12, 2006 letter to the Walla Walla Union-Bulletin, titled "Don't Bend Walla Walla," saying in part:

> Those who are questioning the Illahee Development by the Bend Company Abito, formerly Pennbrook, are not saying that we should shut the gates in Walla Walla. Given our already rich community culture, we don't believe further growth is something we need to seek, although a certain amount of growth is natural and inevitable. Rather than saying "no growth," we call for smart growth. Our view is that if new people want to come to Walla Walla, they should respect our community, including its downtown and residential districts, and should locate in designated urban growth areas, not in our open fields. New development should also accommodate all income levels, rather than devoting the bulk of new residential land and projects to overbuilt homes for wealthy people to the detriment of low and middle-income residents.
>
> Illahee will take some of our best farmland, utilize scarce water for another golf course as well as second homes, leapfrog beyond other urban development, and subvert our local comprehensive plan and agreed roles of local governmental agencies.
>
> Good lessons are to be learned from smart growth projects around the country. Illahee doesn't represent smart growth. It illustrates the harm an out-of-town company can create when seeking to exploit an attractive community for its own profit.
>
> On behalf of Walla Walla 2020, I'd like to invite you to join us in working for sustainability and smart growth policies for the Walla Walla area.

# 2. A Water Rights Complaint

In order to provide the water needed for Illahee's golf course and luxury homes, in addition to the Port's existing deep well which extended into Walla Walla's diminishing basalt aquifer, the Port's plan was to acquire two more deep wells on farmland adjoining the airport. To provide funding for these acquisitions the Port applied for two grants from the Federal Aviation Administration based on its representations to the FAA that these lands were needed for runway protection purposes, while it concealed the actual purpose of its planned acquisitions. The Port's grant applications also failed to disclose the source of the matching funds for the grants as required, which were to come from Pennbrook.

Though there were many reasons why Walla Walla 2020 opposed the development, we viewed the water arrangements between the Port and Pennbrook as the project's most serious threat to the well-being of the community.

Walla Walla's deep aquifer had been declining for years, with more water being pumped each year for agriculture, housing, industry, and other purposes than was being naturally replenished. Because of that, Walla Walla had been designated by the state as a Critical Water Supply Service Area, and a Coordinated Water System Plan had been adopted by all local water supply systems. An essential part of the plan required that all water suppliers use water from Mill Creek during the high flow seasons through the City of Walla Walla's surface water right, and that further pumping from the deep aquifer be limited to times when surface waters were unavailable. In addition, the City had begun a successful project of recharging the deep aquifer through the injection of surface water into its deep wells adjacent to the Walla Walla airport during high stream flow.

Instead of complying with the Coordinated Water System Plan, the Port planned to pump and sell water to Pennbrook from the same aquifer block the city was using for its recharge program, potentially defeating the City's efforts to replenish the aquifer.

The Port began its water planning for Illahee by contracting with the Anderson-Perry engineering firm for a study of Port capacity to supply water to the project. When the Port notified local governments of its study, the City of Walla Walla expressed concern about the effect the Port's groundwater withdrawals for the project would have on the City's aquifer recharge program, and requested that the study also look at the potential for City water to be supplied to the development from the City's combined surface and ground water supplies as required by existing water planning policies.

In July 2004, Anderson-Perry issued a report concluding that the Port needed an additional water source to supply Pennbrook. A primary focus of the report was on the adjoining farm owned by Anderson-Perry manager and engineer Keith Olson who initially worked on the study, and who had purchased the farm and water right in 1998 "for investment purposes." Following the Anderson-Perry report, Olson proposed to sell his farm and deep aquifer well to the Port.

Since the Port's primary purpose was to acquire the needed water right, it then began an analysis of how much of the original water right still existed under Washington State's five-year "use it or lose it" relinquishment rule. The rule, codified in Revised Code of Washington section 90.14.180, states,

> Any person hereafter entitled to divert or withdraw waters of the state…who abandons the same, or who voluntarily fails, without sufficient cause, to beneficially use all or any part of said right to withdraw for any period of five successive years shall relinquish such right or portion thereof, and such right or portion thereof shall revert to the state…

Although sugar beets were grown on a portion of the Olson farm in the 1950's through the mid-1970's apparently utilizing the full water right, for over 20 years from the mid-1970's through 1998 the property was primarily devoted to dry land crops, and both the capacity and use of the irrigation system were decreased.

When Olson purchased the property he immediately installed a new pump to increase water use, and in 2002 instructed his farm tenant to plant 100 acres of alfalfa in order to justify winter irrigation and to further increase water usage. In early 2004, about the time the Port asked Anderson-Perry and Olson as its Walla Walla manager to do a feasibility study on providing water to Pennbrook, Olson instructed his farm tenant to pump 100% of his certificated right during the year 2004, even though that exceeded the amount needed for his crops and exceeded the remaining unrelinquished portion of his water entitlement.

In 2004 and early 2005, the Port and Olson entered into purchase negotiations centering on the value of the water right, the degree of relinquishment, and the amount of the remaining right that might be transferable to municipal use to serve Pennbrook, which had agreed to contribute funds for the purchase of the property. On September 30, 2005, the Port purchased the Olson farm and deep well with the FAA runway protection funds it had applied for together with money from Pennbrook.

On the closing of the sale, the Port immediately began implementing its own plans to increase water consumption from the well through the planting of 200 additional acres of alfalfa and by installing a new pumping and irrigation system with increased capacity.

On June 14, 2006, representatives of Walla Walla 2020 including a Walla Walla College hydrologist met with the Port of Walla Walla's executive director to discuss evidence 2020 had collected regarding the partial relinquishment of the Olson water right as well as partial relinquishment of the adjoining water right on the Frazier farm which the Port was also in the process of acquiring. The 2020 representatives stated their objections to what they understood to be the Port's plan to unlawfully pump water for the irrigation of 300 acres of alfalfa on the Olson farm, an amount in excess of the remaining water right for the property. In response, the Port executive confirmed the Port's intention to pump at the maximum certificated rate until such time as an application is made by the Port for a transfer of its water rights to municipal purposes at some undetermined time in the future.

In response, on September 18, 2006, Walla Walla 2020 and three adjoining farm neighbors filed a complaint with the Washington State Department of Ecology alleging intentional violation of water rights by the Port, and attached documentation including the original water rights certificate for the Olson well, a statement by the farm tenant regarding Olson's instructions to him, cropping records for the property, and power company records showing pump use for the property from which the actual pumping history can be calculated. A copy of the complaint itself is attached as Appendix D.

The Department of Ecology responded by letter of October 13, 2006 informing the Port of the complaint, and advising the Port that water usage for the Olson well "should be consistent with those quantities historically withdrawn and used to irrigate" the land, and that its water right certificate is limited to a designated season.

On February 24, 2007, Walla Walla 2020 again wrote to Ecology, stating:

> We are writing on behalf of our organization and several neighbors of the Port of Walla Walla as a follow-up to our September 16, 2006 letter of complaint regarding water abuse by the Port.
>
> We appreciate your October 13, 2006 letter to the Port informing it of this complaint, advising it that water usage for the Olson well "should be consistent with those quantities historically withdrawn and used to irrigate" this farm, and that the water right certificate is limited to a designated season.
>
> We have now completed a detailed analysis of the use of this water right, #3863-A, based on past power records and other data. Our analysis shows that the maximum beneficial use to which this water right was put for the period 1999-2005 was less than 1/3 of the 1050 acre feet per year shown on the certificate. As you know, the use of this right is limited to the period from May 1 to November 30 each year, and water use for this 521 acre farm cannot lawfully be spread beyond the 300 acre limitation contained in the certificate.
>
> The farm records we have provided you show that this ground had not been planted to alfalfa prior to 2002 when the Olsons planted alfalfa on approximately 100 acres. This was increased by them to approximately 150 acres of alfalfa in 2004, and has since been increased by the Port to 300 acres of alfalfa.
>
> The power company records we have provided you for the pump on this farm clearly demonstrate the unlawful pumping of water by the Olsons beginning in 2002 and by the Port of Walla Walla beginning in 2005, both by illegally pumping beyond the authorized season and by pumping in quantities that clearly exceed the remaining unrelinquished amount of this right.
>
> We have requested complete past records for the water meter we understand has been installed on the Olson well, as well as future monthly readings. These records will allow us to monitor current water use, and to compare power records to further confirm our analysis regarding past usage.
>
> As the 2007 irrigation season approaches, we will be providing you and the Port our analysis of the remaining water right, and will be monitoring whether additional unlawful pumping occurs. If it does, we will be requesting that Ecology take immediate action to protect the rights of neighboring users and municipal water supplies from this abuse.
>
> In the meantime, we can provide further details regarding our analysis, on request.

On June 27, 2007 the Department of Ecology further notified the complainants that at such time as the Port files a change of use application for the water right the Department will evaluate all the information provided and make a determination as to the extent and validity of the Port's remaining rights.

# 3. A Complaint to the FAA

On May 18, 2006, Walla Walla 2020 gave the Federal Aviation Administration notice of its concerns about misrepresentation and concealment in the Port's runway protection grant applications, and began a series of public records requests to both the Port and the FAA in order to obtain documentary evidence of their relevant actions. A copy of 2020's May 18 letter is attached as Appendix A.

After reviewing hundreds of records, including emails, letters, reports, grant applications, and related documents, Walla Walla 2020 prepared the lengthy chronology of Port and FAA actions concerning the Illahee project which is set out as Appendix C, to which it attached nearly 400 pages of corroborating documents. The group then sent this chronology with all attachments to the FAA along with a formal complaint alleging intentional misrepresentation and concealment by the Port and misfeasance and collusion by FAA staff.

The Walla Walla 2020 complaint of August 21, 2006, included as Appendix B, stated in part:

> The public records from the FAA and the Port of Walla Walla provide clear evidence of a course of intentional misrepresentation, omission, and concealment with respect to both grant applications and grant agreements.
>
> The chronology we have prepared is attached, together with a full analysis of the misrepresentations and omissions in each grant application.
>
> The information shows that at the same time the Port represented to the FAA that these grants were needed for runway protection, it was telling the developers and local interests that it intended to use these purchases to provide water for the planned residential development. In addition, the developers agreed to pay and have paid the Port $422,175 toward the purchase price of the property, which was not disclosed to the FAA.
>
> In view of this misrepresentation and concealment, as well as the apparent collusion of FAA staff, we are requesting a thorough review of both grant proceedings by appropriate authorities, and that appropriate steps be taken to protect the interest of the United States and its taxpayers, prior to the payout of any further federal funds.

On October 27, 2006, after a thorough review and investigation of the complaint, the Federal Aviation Administration responded by issuing seventy-one pages of findings, available in their entirety online at . Its key findings are quoted or summarized below.

1. The Port of Walla Walla "misrepresented or concealed" the objective, benefits, and parties involved in its application for federal funds to purchase the 521 acre Olson farm and its deep aquifer well. Misrepresentation is defined by the FAA as "material misrepresentation of presently existing or past fact, made with knowledge of its falsity and with intention that another party rely thereon, resulting in reliance by that party to his detriment." Concealment is defined by

the FAA as "the withholding of information which one in honesty and good faith is bound to reveal."

2.  A major objective of the Olson acquisition "was the need for Pennbrook to obtain water for its development and the Port's desire to provide water as a revenue source."

"Four months prior to discussing the Olson property purchase with the FAA, the Port entered into numerous conversations with Pennbrook regarding the supply of water. During this time the Port received an initial assessment that the Port's current water supply was not sufficient to support Pennbrook. Prior to submitting its grant application, (the) Port entered into negotiations with Pennbrook to accept $422,175 for the purchase of the Olson farm in consideration of supplying water."

"…The Port presented to the FAA numerous justifications for the purchase including RPZ, MANPADS, 50:1 transitional zone, and uneconomic remnants. On four occasions during the application period there was an opportunity to provide the FAA with an accurate representation of the Port's interest in supplying water…"

"The Port never informed the FAA of its pending agreement with Pennbrook to accept payment with the condition of supplying water. Instead, the Port continued to mislead the FAA that the primary use of the water was for the industrial park."

3.  "FAA officials failed to comply with FAA rules requiring disposal of land that is unneeded for airport protection purposes on both the Olson and the 263 acre Frazier farm acquisition grants….the Port of Walla Walla is out of compliance with the grant provision requiring such disposal…Failure to come into compliance could result in withholding of further FAA funds and a further investigation of the Port."

4.  FAA officials were also found to have failed to comply with the FAA's environmental review requirements for land acquisition for both the Olson and Frazier grants. While the Olson grant has been paid out and closed, an FAA environmental review of the Frazier grant is to be conducted, and the Port of Walla Walla will be obligated to mitigate any significant impacts identified as a grant condition.

5.  The Port of Walla Walla was also found to have intentionally concealed public objections to the Olson grant and to have failed to disclose those objections to the FAA as required by FAA rules. FAA officials were themselves found to have failed to respond to citizen objections made directly to the FAA as required by FAA guidelines, and the officials involved were ordered to respond to all citizen complaints it had received regarding both grants.

Because the misrepresentation and concealment described amounted to criminal fraud punishable as a felony, following receipt of the findings the Port hired an east coast lawyer to appeal the findings to the FAA's top administrator. While not retracting the findings of misrepresentation, the FAA then issued a further inconsistent statement that no criminal fraud was determined to have occurred, thereby defusing the issue of criminal misconduct.

# 4. The Environmental Appeal

Despite the fact that the proposed Illahee project would be the largest development in Walla Walla County history, that its location was dangerously close to two airport runways and to two hazardous chlorine storage areas, and that its water was to come exclusively from our declining aquifer, the County determined that it would have no significant impact on the environment. This determination meant that Pennbrook would not be required to prepare an Environmental Impact Statement (EIS) under the State Environmental Policy Act (SEPA), RCW Chapter 43.21C.

On June 29, 2006, Walla Walla 2020 and Citizens for Good Governance both appealed the County's decision. Among the SEPA criteria for determining whether an EIS should be prepared is the extent of controversy concerning a project. In 2006, letters critical of the Pennbrook/Port project were published in the Walla Walla Union-Bulletin on January 8, 15, 29 and 30, and on February 5, 10, and 12. In addition, from February 19-24 the newspaper published twenty-three different articles on the controversy raised by the Port's water plans, including expressions of concern by farm neighbors, environmentalists, water experts, public officials, and other citizens.

After both the county hearing examiner and the board of county commissioners rejected our appeals, Walla Walla 2020 then filed an appeal in superior court naming Walla Walla County and Pennbrook as respondents.

The impacts raised in the Walla Walla 2020 appeal included:

1. Serious threats to the area's water supply systems.

2. Deadly risks to Illahee residents relating to potential catastrophic leaks from the City's chlorine water treatment plant and the McGregor Company's anhydrous ammonia storage facility, both directly adjacent to and upwind of the site, as well as the Wilbur-Ellis anhydrous ammonia facility nearby.

3. The impact of the exclusively second home and luxury housing planned at Illahee on the availability and cost of housing for low and moderate income residents which is increasingly in short supply.

4. The risks of locating new high-density housing within the airport's accident safety zone for two of its runways.

5. Impacts to the area's ground transportation system, including additional risks to bicyclists, pedestrians, and motorists accessing the project from the south on a two-lane road without sidewalks, bike lanes or shoulders, as well as the lack of transit service to the project.

These impacts are discussed in detail in the appellant's appeal brief which is set out in Appendix D in its entirety. Following the filing of the brief, and the judge's appointment of a mediator to assist the parties, a settlement was entered into by all of the parties to the litigation.

# 5. The Outcome

Under the terms of the settlement reached by all parties to the appeal, the developer was required to annex the project property into the city of Walla Walla, and to obtain all water for the project from the city's dual-source water supply system, rather than from the Port of Walla Walla. Additional favorable terms included in the settlement were not disclosed.

The planned golf course was ultimately dropped from the project by the developer. In addition, following a severe downturn in the national economy the Illahee project itself was abandoned, and the property has been returned to the farm family from which Pennbrook purchased it.

At present this farm land is still in wheat production, and continues to yield 125 bushels a year with no irrigation other than the natural rainfall. Also, a critical portion of the Walla Walla area's deep aquifer has been protected from threatened depletion by the project, and is continuing to be replenished by the City of Walla Walla's aquifer recharge program. And, at least for now, sprawling development that was planned towards our beautiful Blue Mountains has been halted.

The future will undoubtedly hold additional challenges for our community.

# Appendix A: Inquiry to the Federal Aviation Administration

## WALLA WALLA 2020

May 18, 2006

Jeff Winter
Federal Aviation Administration
1601 Lind Ave, SW, Suite 250
Seattle WA

Re:  Walla Walla Airport Acquisition Grants

Dear Mr. Winter:

As I explained by telephone today, the Walla Walla 2020 citizens group is interested in the recent and pending farmland acquisition grant applications by the Port of Walla Walla for the Olson and Frazier properties north of the Walla Walla Airport, and would like to receive copies of all related correspondence and grant documents, as well as citations of applicable standards.

As you are aware, the Port has recently involved itself in the facilitation of a highly controversial residential development on productive farmland adjacent to the airport, including agreements to supply water for the development from Port groundwater, as well as sewer services.  Part of the community-wide controversy is related to the Port's plan to pump groundwater for the development from a well drawing from the same aquifer in which the city of Walla Walla is injecting recharge water due to continual aquifer decline.

In this context, we are concerned that the proposed and completed acquisition of farm properties containing wells and acreage considerably beyond appropriate runway protection needs may be driven in large part by residential development motives rather than solely FAA eligible purposes.

Under these circumstances, including the high profile of the controversy over the Port's actions in this matter, we suggest that an outside panel be asked to review the appropriateness of the acquisition and retention proposals by the Port with regard to the Olson and Frazier properties in the context of accepted runway protection standards before any further action is taken by FAA with respect to these properties.

We look forward to receiving the requested documents and citations, as well as your response to the proposal for a further review of these matters before further FAA action.

Sincerely,

Daniel N. Clark
Project Coordinator
clarkdn@charter.net

cc:  Jim Kuntz, Port of Walla Walla

# Appendix B: Complaint to the Federal Aviation Administration

## WALLA WALLA 2020

August 21, 2006

Douglas Murphy
Regional Administrator
Federal Aviation Administration
Northwest Mountain Region
1601 Lind Avenue Southwest
Renton, Washington 98055

Re: Walla Walla Airport Acquisition Grants
      Frazier and Olson farms

Dear Mr. Murphy:

We wrote to the FAA on May 18, 2006 regarding our concerns about misrepresentations by the Port of Walla Walla for the purpose of qualifying for two FAA land acquisition grants intended for airport runway protection. As the attached chronology shows, contrary to the representations of the Port, the primary purpose of these acquisitions is to supply water to the proposed Pennbrook residential development adjacent to the Walla Walla Regional Airport.

The enclosed chronology also demonstrates that the Port has omitted and concealed other relevant and critical information in its two grant applications. In particular, the Port has failed to provide any information on citizen opposition to its highly controversial plans, as required by the grant documents.

In view of this misrepresentation and concealment, as well as the apparent collusion of FAA staff, we are requesting a thorough review of both grant proceedings by appropriate authorities, and that appropriate steps be taken to protect the interest of the United States and its taxpayers, prior to the payout of any further federal funds.

The information below shows that at the same time the Port represented to the FAA that these grants were needed for runway protection, it was telling the developers and local interests that it intended to use these purchases to provide water for the planned residential development. In addition, the developers agreed to pay and have paid $422,175 towards the Port's share of the purchase price of the initial property.

The first grant took place on July 14, 2005, when the FAA made an award to the Port of Walla Walla for the purchase of the Olson property, a large farm with a deep well north of the Walla Walla Regional Airport. On June 6, 2006 the FAA made a similar grant award to the Port of Walla Walla for the purchase of the Frazier property, another large farm with a deep well north of the airport. Each of these grants included large portions of land acknowledged to be unneeded for runway protection purposes. Neither grant was conditioned on resale and deduction of unneeded portions, as required by Order 5100.38C, Airport Improvement Program Handbook, paragraph 702. In addition, neither grant appears to have complied with the environmental steps required by Order 1050.1E, paragraphs 303-312.

The public records provided to this point by the FAA and the Port of Walla Walla provide clear evidence of a course of intentional misrepresentation, omission, and concealment with respect to both the grant applications and grant agreements. To assist you and others in the review of this documentary evidence, we have prepared a chronology summarizing the actions of the Port of Walla Walla, FAA staff, and others regarding the acquisition of these properties. Further public record requests have been made to both agencies, and we hope in the future to be able to provide additional documentation and analysis regarding this course of conduct.

A copy of the chronology we have prepared is attached, together with a full analysis of the misrepresentations and omissions in each grant application. The underlying documents are available at http://www.wallawalla2020.org/pennbrook_chronology_documents_8-20-06.pdf.

The records referenced in the chronology document the following sequence of events:

1. The 2002 Airport Layout Plan Update for the Walla Walla Regional Airport recommends acquisition of 60.6 acres northeast of runway 20 for the protection of the runway, and in 2003 the Port of Walla Walla prioritizes the project as the last priority in its six year capital projects report, targeted for 2009.

2. In early 2004, the Port of Walla Walla begins discussions with Pennbrook Homes, a Bend, Oregon developer, regarding supply of water by the Port to a residential development proposed by Pennbrook on farmland east of the airport, and Pennbrook agrees to fund consultants to be hired by the Port to handle design, permitting, and other legal and engineering requirements for the Port to supply water and other services to the development.

3. The Port contracts with Anderson-Perry & Associates, Inc, to perform the utility study. The study concludes that for the Port to supply water to Pennbrook, a new water source will be required, and identifies the deep well on the Keith Olson farm northeast of the airport as the primary focus. The Frazier farm west of Olson appears to have been a secondary focus. A new reservoir will also be required, which the report proposes be located on the Olson property.

4. In May, 2004, Olson, an Anderson-Perry engineer and hydrologist, offers to sell the property and well to the Port. He had purchased the 521-acre farm and well in 1997 for $765,000, and offers to sell it to the Port for $2,587,100, based in large part on the value of its water rights.

5. In June-July, 2004, the Port executive tells FAA officials that purchase of the Olson property is needed for runway protection, despite an existing runway protection easement, and that its well is needed for industrial purposes. No mention is made of the Pennbrook project, or of the possibility of protecting the runway through a further easement. During the same period, the Port executive writes to the Walla Walla city manager regarding Olson, "This is an active high production well. It will likely supply all the water needs of Pennbrook and may help the airport industrial park accommodate future growth."

6. In August, 2004, the Port drafts, submits, and begins lobbying for proposed changes in local comprehensive plan policies to eliminate language against housing encroachment in the vicinity of the airport, and to permit the Port to be the water supplier for new residential development near the airport.

7. Also in August, 2004, FAA officials evaluate the Port's acquisition request, term its security justification "weak" as well as its non-compatibility argument in view of the 40 acre minimum lot zoning, and tell the Port that at most only 35% of the property is eligible for Airport Improvement Program funds. The Port responds the same month with a request that FAA cover 87% of the property, with the Port to pay the balance "with its own resources."

8. In February, 2005, the Port tells the FAA that its "willingness to contribute not less than $306,054 to acquire this property is an indication of our interest in protecting the airport's main runway from incompatible land uses." No mention is made of the negotiations with Pennbrook to pay the Port's share of the purchase price of the property.

9. In April, 2005, FAA official Jeff Winter is informed by a citizen watchdog of the connection between the Port's interest in the Olson farm and the Pennbrook development. In a communication to the Port executive, Winter refers to Pennbrook as "a non-compatible use," and states "it was our earlier understanding from you that the water rights would be used to develop the on-airport industrial park." In a 4-22-05 response, the Port executive requests help with the airport's financial problems.

10. In May, 2005, the Port executive assures FAA regarding the property that the "water right will be used for airport industrial park purposes…the airport as a utility provider may also supply water to developments near the airport." The day after this assurance, the Port confirmed with Pennbrook its understanding that in exchange for Pennbrook's contribution of $422,175 to the Olson purchase price, Pennbrook would receive a portion of the Olson water right or a portion of the Olson property if Pennbrook's development project did not proceed.

11. In an email on May 11, 2005, responding to the Port's plea for help with the financial condition of the airport, FAA official Jeff Winter advises the Port on how to increase the amount of its appraisal to justify the higher price the seller is demanding. Winter also withdraws his requirement that the ineligible portion of the Olson land be sold off.

12. On June 20, 2005, city and county planning commissions hold a joint hearing on changes to planning policies proposed by the Port and Pennbrook to facilitate Pennbrook and future residential development around the airport. A variety of citizens object to the proposals and to Pennbrook, citing water and other environmental concerns, encroachment of residential development on the airport, sprawl, and loss of farmland, among other matters; the hearing is featured in a lead article in the local newspaper. The city council then debates the matter, and the local newspaper editorializes about it.

13. On June 24, 2005, the Port advises the FAA it has agreed to buy the Olson property for $1,950,000, contingent on funding by the FAA. No mention is made of a further contingency of funding by Pennbrook. On July 11, 2005, the Port signs a purchase and sale agreement on the Olson property, contingent on funding by both FAA and Pennbrook.

14. On July 12, 2005, the Port executive files a grant application with the FAA for Olson purchase funds, containing a variety of intentional misrepresentations. The application does not disclose the property's relationship to the Pennbrook project and the payment to be made by Pennbrook, falsely states the project is consistent with existing comprehensive plans, states it will have no environmental effects without discussion or analysis, and conceals information on citizen objections. See the attached full analysis of misrepresentations in the 7-12-05 application.

15. On July 14, 2005, the FAA awards a grant to the Port for the Olson acquisition in the amount of $1,457,946. No special condition is included requiring sale of the portion of the property unneeded for runway protection. The grant was accepted by the Port on July 27, 2005. The purchase has since closed and the grant funds have been disbursed.

16. In September, 2005, Port officials tell the FAA the owners of the Frazier farm and deep well located next to Olson also want to sell to the Port. The FAA responds that the farm land excess to runway protection needs to be sold to finance the purchase of qualifying runway protection land.

17. In February, 2006, a lead article in the Walla Walla newspaper reports on the Port's negotiations with Pennbrook as to details for supplying water to the development, followed by a letter to the editor, and a week-long series of 23 articles focusing on what is becoming the community's highest profile controversy, including concerns by farm neighbors, environmentalists, water experts, officials, and other citizens. These concerns

are further expressed by the delivery of petitions to the Port and other agencies signed by over 800 people opposing the project.

18.  On March 20, 2006, the Port signs an option agreement to purchase the 261.7 acre Frazier farm and well for $1,151,480.  The next day Port officials provide a public PowerPoint presentation and handout demonstrating the relationship of the Frazier and Olson wells to the Pennbrook project.  This relationship is confirmed in a slide show and handout by the Port for a community tour on June 9, 2006, captioning both the Olson property and the Olson and Frazier wells as "Illahee Project" the formal name for the development.

19.  On May 1, 2006, Port executive Jim Kuntz files a grant application with the FAA for the Frazier purchase, containing a variety of intentional misrepresentations and omissions including the concealment of information as to citizen objections and the property's relationship to the Pennbrook project.  See the attached detailed analysis of misrepresentations in the 5-1-06 application.

20.  On May 3, 2006, the FAA requests justification for purchase of the entire Frazier farm, since the land is already protected by an aviation easement, and 53% of it is beyond the allowed area for runway protection.  The same day, the FAA receives a request for information on the grant from a neighboring farm family, followed by detailed protests on the absence of hearings and environmental review, farmer displacements, water supply motives v. runway protection, price inflation, and the Port's planting and watering of alfalfa to build up its water right claim to the detriment of neighboring wells.

21.  On May 8, 2006, the FAA tells the Port the Frazier grant will likely be conditioned on a requirement that both the Frazier and Olson excess land be resold by the Port, with the proceeds used to fund an eligible project.  The next day, the FAA cites FAA Order 5100.38C, ¶ 702 on requirements for the sale of unneeded property.

22.  On May 18, 2006, Walla Walla 2020 writes to FAA official Jeff Winter raising concerns about all of these matters, requesting an outside review of the appropriateness of the Port's acquisition and retention proposals before further FAA action on the pending proposals, and requesting copies of all relevant documents.  The FAA responded by providing requested documentation, and advising that our outside review request would be addressed by separate correspondence.

23.  On July 14, 2006, the FAA's Seattle office awards the Port a grant of $1,118,095 for the purchase of the 262 acre Frazier farm and well, with no resale requirements for the portions of either the Frazier or Olson property that are unneeded for runway zone protection.  This grant is further made without responding to Walla Walla 2020's review request, or notice of the intended or actual award.  The extent of any environmental assessment is unknown.

This chronology shows the intentional misrepresentations, omissions, and concealment of Port of Walla Walla officials, as well as the failure of FAA staff to comply with FAA standards, regulations, and procedures for the protection of the public.

Special condition No. 9 in the grant agreements provides that "if, during the life of the project, the FAA determines that a change in the grant description is advantageous and in the best interests of the United States, the change in grant description will be unilaterally amended by letter from the FAA."

Section 1027 of FAA Order 5100.38C, provides: The region may rescind the acceptance of sponsor certification forms at any time. Where fraud or criminal action and intent is suspected, the U.S. Justice Department shall be immediately notified through regional counsel.

While the Olson purchase has closed and been funded, it is our understanding that the Frazier purchase is scheduled for closing later this month, and that FAA funds have not been paid out on that grant. Prior to any payout on the grant, a thorough review of both grant proceedings should be undertaken by appropriate authorities, and remedial action should be taken to protect the interest of the United States and its taxpayers.

We request your immediate acknowledgment of this letter, as well as notification of the steps you intend to take with respect to the issues raised.

Sincerely,

Daniel N. Clark
V.P. & Project Coordinator
clarkdn@charter.net

cc:    Marion C. Blakey, FAA National Administrator
       Andy Steinberg, FAA Chief Counsel
       Carl B. Lewis, FAA Regional Counsel
       Department of Transportation Inspector General
       Government Accountability Office

# Appendix C:
# Chronology, Port of Walla Walla-Illahee Project

**09-01-98\*  Moore Farm put up for sale**
The Moore Farm, 521 acres adjoining the Walla Walla Regional Airport on the northeast, is put up for sale, including one of the few deep water wells in the Walla Walla-College Place area The listing documents show the farm's 10-year history of dry-land cropping.

**10-01-98\*  Olson buys Moore Farm for $765,000**
Keith Olson, an engineer, hydrologist, and manager of a local engineering office, buys the Moore Farm "for investment purposes," pays $765,000, and leases it to a local farmer. Olson installs new pump and begins to increase water use over prior levels.

**09-01-03\*  Port sets 2009 as target for purchase of 60 acres of Moore Farm**
In its aviation capital projects report for 2003, the Port of Walla prioritizes projects at the Walla Walla Regional Airport for the following six years. Acquisition of 60.6 acres in the Runway 20 approach area, including about 4 acres on the Moore/Olson farm, is its last priority, targeted for 2009.

**10-01-03\*  Pennbrook site proposal submitted to city**
Pennbrook Homes, a Bend, Oregon developer, proposes to develop a large site adjoining the Walla Walla airport as a resort and housing project; the landowner and developer contact city officials regarding permits and provision of city water and sewer to the site, and the city gives notice of the proposal to other agencies.

**12-26-03  Port expresses concern about Pennbrook**
Port of Walla Walla executive Jim Kuntz writes to the city expressing concerns about potential conflicts between residential development at the Pennbrook site and present and future industrial and aeronautic activities at the airport.

**03-01-04\*  Port and Pennbrook discuss water supply, Port advises against annexation**
Pennbrook and Port executive discuss the Port supplying water for Pennbrook by pumping from the Port's existing well, and possibly through purchase of an additional water right from the distant Ash Hollow area. Kuntz advises Pennbrook against annexing the site to the city.

**03-01-04\*  Pennbrook approaches county, advises of Port discussions**
Pennbrook approaches county development director regarding county approvals, and advises of water supply discussions with Port.

**03-31-04  Port, Pennbrook consult Anderson-Perry for evaluation of water supply, Olson responds**
On 3-24-04, Port and Pennbrook officials contact Olson, manager of Anderson-Perry, engineers, for an evaluation of the Port's capacity to supply water for the Pennbrook development. On 3-31-04, Olson sends a preliminary response to the Port, and on 4-29-04 provides a scope of work.

**05-01-04\*  Olson proposes sale of farm and well to Port**
Olson proposes to Port officials a possible sale of his farm property and well to the Port for $2,587,100, as a source of water for the Pennbrook development, and instructs his farm tenant to pump water beyond the normal irrigation season.

**05-26-04  Port signs agreement with Pennbrook to pay for consultant services**
On 5-26-04, Port executive Jim Kuntz signed an agreement with Pennbrook providing for hiring of legal and engineering consultants at Pennbrook's expense to handle design, permitting, water rights, and other legal and engineering requirements for the Port's provision of water and sewer utilities to Pennbrook. On 6-9-04, the Port commissioners approve the agreement, which is renewed on 5-25-05.

**06-14-04  Port formally contracts with Anderson-Perry for utilities study, notifies local governments**
On 6-14-04, Port executive signed a contract with Anderson-Perry to perform the Pennbrook feasibility study. He also notifies the city and county of the study.

**06-28-04\*  City expresses concerns, requests that study include city water supply for project**
On 6-28-04, city manager Duane Cole writes to the Port, requesting that the Pennbrook utility study also include options for water supply by the city, and expresses concerns that groundwater withdrawal by the Port for Pennbrook would undermine the city's nearby aquifer recharge program, and that the Port and Pennbrook would be benefiting from that program as well as from the city's emergency intertie without contributing to their costs. The study is not expanded.

**07-01-04\*  Anderson-Perry draft says Olson well is needed to supply Pennbrook**
Anderson-Perry issues a draft of its Water and Sewer Utilities Assessment, dated July, 2004. The draft, under discussion for several months, concludes that a new water source and an additional reservoir will be needed for the Port to supply water to Pennbrook, and focuses on the Olson property and well as the primary means to accomplish this. Unnamed secondary water sources are also studied.

**07-01-04\*  Port tells FAA that Olson property needed for runway protection & industrial purposes**
On 6-22-06, Port executive meets with Federal Aviation Administration official and discusses the need to purchase the Olson property to protect Runway 02, already protected by an aviation easement obtained in 1959. On 6-30-04, Kuntz writes to the Walla Walla city manager regarding the Olson farm, saying, "If we purchase the property a substantial water right will come with it. This is an active high production well. It will likely supply all the water needs of Pennbrook and may help the airport industrial park accommodate future growth." On 7-23-06, Kuntz writes to the FAA that the 40 acre zoning for the property presents the risk of incompatible residential development, that hand-held missiles could be fired from the property, and that its well is needed for Port industrial purposes. The Port's interest in providing water for residential development is not disclosed to the FAA, nor does the Port propose the alternative of securing any needed runway protection through additional easements.

**08-01-04\*  Port seeks to eliminate planning policies against housing in vicinity of airport**
To facilitate the Pennbrook development, the Port drafts, submits, and begins lobbying for proposed changes to Walla Walla County's comprehensive plan policies to eliminate prohibitions against housing encroachment in the vicinity of the airport, and to permit the Port to be the water supplier for nearby residential development.

**08-01-04\*  FAA tells Port most of Olson property ineligible for funding, asks about water rights**
The FAA evaluates the Port's request for funding to acquire the Olson farm, and notes the Port's national security justification is "weak," as is its argument that 40 acre zoning is incompatible with the airport. On 8-3-04, in a conference call between FAA and Port officials, the FAA informs the Port that, at most, 180 acres (35%) of the Olson property is eligible for funding. In an 8-18-04 letter response, the Port requests that FAA cover 87% of the property, with the Port paying for the

balance "with its own resources." On 8-24-04, FAA requests additional justification for the Port's request, including details on the projected revenue benefit to the Port from the water right.

**10-01-04\*  Port obtains $1,764,000 appraisal on Olson farm, Olson wants $2,313,800, mostly for water**

> The Port orders an appraisal of the Olson property. The appraisal is completed on 10-21-04, and shows a market value of $1,764,000. Olson's asking price is now $2,313,800, attributing 62% to the water right and well, as shown in an Illahee cost analysis prepared by the Port and in negotiation documents prepared by the Port and Olson, which recognize that a significant portion of the water right has been relinquished through non-use.

**01-01-05\*  Pennbrook and Port pressure city to allow use of Olson well for Pennbrook**

> In early January, 2005, Pennbrook and Anderson-Perry officials meet with City of Walla Walla staff; city water manager Robert Gordon expresses concern about use of the Olson well for Pennbrook because of potential conflicts with the city's aquifer recharge program for its public water supply system. On 1-7-05, Gordon tells Anderson-Perry he wants future Olson well usage to be no more than current usage and asks for data on current usage of the well. Anderson-Perry diverts the question, saying that would be considered at the time of conversion from farm use, and that the Port executive and its lawyer would be working on that. The Port executive then advises Pennbrook to go around Gordon to the city manager to obtain agreement on Olson well and other requirements for the Port to supply water to Pennbrook, and also recommends that the Port's lawyer draft a letter from Pennbrook to the city for Pennbrook to approve and sign. Pennbrook notes it is clear the city wants to supply water for the project, and asks the Port executive to talk to the city manager, who Pennbrook says "needs to call off his dogs."

**02-01-05\*   Port changes Olson property to #1 priority, FAA tells Port some of Olson property has to be sold**

> In his letter of 2-1-05, Port executive tells the FAA that acquisition of the Olson property for protection of runway 20 is now the Port's #1 capital priority for 2005, and that "the Port's willingness to contribute not less than $306,054 to acquire this property is an indication of our interest in protecting the airport's main runway from incompatible land uses." In responding to the FAA question about revenue benefits to the Port from the water right, Kuntz fails to disclose the Port's intention to provide water for the Pennbrook residential development, and acknowledges the probable relinquishment of 20-25% of the right from non-use. In a response dated 2-10-05, the FAA gives the Port permission to proceed with a review appraisal with the understanding that a portion of the Olson property would have to be resold by the Port to satisfy FAA guidelines.

**3-25-05  Pennbrook formally offers to pay part of Olson price for Port operation of water system**

> On 3-25-05, Pennbrook officials write to the Port formally offering to contribute $422,175 toward the Port's share of the expected Olson acquisition costs. Pennbrook prefers that the Port manage the water system for the Illahee development, but is willing to go along with the Port's desire that the system be privately operated by Illahee with wholesale water from the Port, which the Port is to provide at 30% of city rates.

**04-01-05\*   FAA learns about Pennbrook, questions Port regarding inconsistent statements**

> The FAA is alerted by a citizen to the connection between the Olson property and Pennbrook, which the FAA refers to as "a non-compatible use" in a 4-22-05 email to the Port executive, adding "it was our earlier understanding from you that the water rights would be used to develop the on-airport industrial park." In a 4-22-05 written response, Kuntz denies that Pennbrook is a non-compatible land use (despite its violation of the airport's existing master plan), and asks FAA help with the airport's financial problems.

**05-10-05   Port tells FAA it wants to keep all of Olson property, stresses value of water**
In a letter to the FAA dated 5-10-05, the Port executive seeks to keep all of the Olson property. Kuntz stresses the value of the water right, and the Port's intention to change it to municipal use, saying, "The municipal water right will be used for airport industrial park purposes.  As mentioned in my April 22 email, the airport as a utility provider may also supply water to developments near the airport as a way to generate additional revenue for the airport."

**05-11-05   Port confirms water agreement with Pennbrook including contribution to Olson purchase**
On 5-11-05, the Port writes to Pennbrook setting out the terms of their "non-binding agreement" for Pennbrook's payment of $422,175 towards the purchase of the Olson property, with Pennbrook to receive a portion of the property or water if the Illahee project can't proceed, and to be required to operate its own private water supply system with wholesale water from the Port.

**05-11-05   FAA official coaches Port on appraisal tactics, relents on excess land and water concerns**
In an email on 5-11-05 responding to the Port's pleas for help with the financial condition of the airport, Jeff Winter, the FAA manager for Walla Walla, coaches Port executive on how to obtain a higher appraisal in order to justify FAA funding of the seller's price.  Winter withdraws his requirement that the ineligible portion of the land be sold off, though he had previously stated "we are not allowed to use AIP funds to acquire land to just create a source of revenue for the airport." He also withdraws his concern regarding the Port providing water to new residential development nearby.

**06-20-05   Citizens object to planning changes proposed by Pennbrook and Port**
On 6-20-05, the city and county planning commissions hold a joint hearing on planning policy changes proposed by the Port and Pennbrook specifically to facilitate the Illahee project.  Various citizens object to the proposed actions and to the Pennbrook project itself. On July 6, the Walla Walla city council also debates the project, and the local newspaper editorializes about it. Port officials are present at both meetings.

**06-24-05\*   Port agrees to buy Olson property at $1,950,000 subject to FAA & Pennbrook funding**
On 6-25-05, the Port notifies the FAA of its agreement to purchase the Olson property for $1,950,000, contingent on an FAA grant. On 6-28-05, the FAA's Winter responds that the FAA will cover the cost of 87% of the property as the Port is requesting.  On 7-11-05, a purchase and sale agreement is executed, contingent not only on FAA funding, but on a $422,175 payment from Pennbrook, and termination of the existing farm lease.

**07-12-05   Port files grant application for Olson property concealing Pennbrook plans and opposition**
On 7-12-05, the Port executive files a grant application with the FAA for funds to purchase the Olson property. The application contains intentional omissions and misrepresentations.

**07-14-05   FAA awards Port $1,457,946 grant for Olson acquisition**
On 7-14-05, the FAA awards a grant to the Port for the Olson acquisition in the amount of $1,457,946 "in consideration of the Sponsor's adoption and ratification of the representations and assurances contained in (the) Project Application." The grant is accepted and the grant agreement executed by the Port executive on 7-27-05.  Grant condition No. 7 states that, "The Sponsor shall take all steps, including litigation if necessary, to recover Federal funds spent fraudulently, wastefully, or in violation of Federal antitrust statutes, or misused in any other manner in any project upon which Federal funds have been expended."  Assurance No. 31(b) provides, "For land purchased under a grant for airport development purposes…(the Sponsor) will, when the land is no longer needed for airport purposes, dispose of such land at fair market value or make available

to the Secretary an amount equal to the United States' proportionate share of the fair market value of the land." No special condition requiring divestment of the unneeded portion of the property is included, despite prior reference to the requirement.

## 09-09-05 Port proposes FAA grant for purchase of Frazier Farm

On 9-9-05, the Port tells the FAA that the owners of the Frazier farm and deep well next to Olson have approached the Port about buying their property. On 9-12-05, the FAA suggests that farm land excess to runway protection be sold to finance the purchase of qualifying runway protection land.

## 09-13-05 Port and Pennbrook execute formal agreement for Olson payment

On 9-13-05, the Port and Pennbrook sign a formal agreement for payment by Pennbrook of $422,175 toward the Olson price, satisfying an express contingency in the purchase and sale agreement for the Olson closing.

## 09-20-05 Port and FAA discuss Olson closing and citizen protests regarding Olson and Pennbrook

On 9-20-05, Port executive Jim Kuntz writes to Jeff Winter of FAA about the planned closing of the Olson purchase on 9-30-05, as well as the request by Walla Walla resident Bud Pringle for all Port files related to Olson and Pennbrook. Winter responds on 9-21-05 that Pringle had contacted him about Pennbrook in March, and that resident Carl Schmitt recently requested FAA documents related to the Olson grant. Special condition No. 9 in the grant agreement gives the FAA power to unilaterally amend the grant provision. Despite these citizen concerns and information about the project's relation to Pennbrook, Winter takes no steps to eliminate the inclusion of excess land prior to the closing of the purchase.

## 10-01-05* Port closes on Olson, plans to increase water consumption from Olson well

The Olson closing is set for 9-30-05, and the Port begins implementing plans to increase water consumption from the Olson well by planting alfalfa and installing a new circle irrigation system in order to maximize its water rights claim for the Pennbrook project.---+

## 11-01-05* Anderson-Perry report details plans to use Olson well for Pennbrook, Port seeks approvals

Consistent with prior drafts, in November 2005 Anderson-Perry issues its final assessment on Port utility service to Pennbrook. The assessment states: "The Port and Pennbrook will use this assessment to proceed with necessary system upgrades and contractual arrangements…The Port of WW desires to maintain available capacity for future industrial uses. However, excess capacity will be made available to Pennbrook on an interim basis. To meet the Port of WW's goal of maintaining existing water capacity for future Port uses, water system improvements must ultimately satisfy 100% of Pennbrook's need…The Port's existing reservoir cannot provide sufficient pressure to the Pennbrook property…The Port of WW has purchased the Moore (Olson) well..The new well will be needed for redundancy before full build-out of the Pennbrook facilities…. Phase 1 improvements are needed for potable water service to Pennbrook…Phase 2 improvements are necessary when Pennbrook will need more than 400 gpm…Phase 2 improvements will generally include rehabilitation at the Moore (Olson) well, a water transmission from the Moore Well to the new ground reservoir, and associated facilities. …Pennbrook will operate a private water distribution system on the Pennbrook site." Consistent with the report, the Port seeks city and county approval to proceed.

## 01-01-06* County approves changes for Pennbrook, critics appeal, Port intervenes

On 10-24-05, the county commissioners approve the various changes in local planning and zoning documents requested by Pennbrook and the Port to facilitate the development; the next day critics announce a likely appeal, which they file on 12-23-05. An additional action is filed by the appellants on 12-28-05; on 1-12-06 the Port announces its intention to intervene in the appeal.

**02-01-06\* Newspaper focuses on Pennbrook and Port water supply controversy**
On 1-8-06, 1-15-06, 1-29-06, 1-30-06, and 2-5-06 opinions critical of the Pennbrook/Port project are published in the Walla Walla Union-Bulletin, and on 2-10-06, a lead article focuses on the Port's negotiations with Pennbrook regarding details of its agreement to supply water for the development, followed by a further letter on 2-12-06. From 2-19-06 through 2-24-06, the paper publishes a total of 23 articles on the controversy surrounding the Port's water plans for Pennbrook, including expressions of concern by farm neighbors, environmentalists, water experts, officials, and other citizens.

**03-14-06 Petitions opposing Pennbrook given to County and Port**
On 3-14-06, petitions opposing Pennbrook signed by over 500 citizens are presented to county commissioners and the Port executive during a meeting with Pennbrook officials. By 4-23-05, petitions totaling over 800 signatures have been delivered to the Port, the county, and the city.

**03-20-06 Port obtains option to purchase Frazier farm for $1,151,480**
On 3-20-06, the Port signs an option agreement with Lester Frazier to purchase his 261.7 acre farm and deep aquifer well adjoining the Olson property for $1,151,480.

**03-21-06 Port officials list Frazier and Olson wells as water resources for Pennbrook**
On 3-21-06, Port executive Jim Kuntz and his assistant present a PowerPoint presentation and handout to a class demonstrating the relationship of the Frazier and Olson wells to the Pennbrook project. This relationship is confirmed in a slide show and handout by the Port for a property tour on 6-9-06, listing the Olson acquisition and the Olson and Frazier wells under the heading "Illahee Project," and also in a letter signed by Kuntz on 4-10-06.

**05-01-06 Port files grant application for Frazier property, concealing development plans & objections**
On 5-1-06, the Port executive files a grant application with the FAA seeking funds to purchase the Frazier farm. The application contains a variety of omissions and misrepresentations.

**05-03-06 FAA tells Port that Frazier property is already protected by airport easement, and that most of it is unneeded for runway protection**
On 5-3-06, the FAA requests justification by the Port for the use of federal funds for purchase of the entire Frazier farm, stating that the land is already protected by an aviation easement, and that 53% of it is beyond the allowed area for runway protection.

**05-03-06 FAA receives inquiry on Frazier grant, rejects objections from farm neighbor**
On 5-3-06, FAA official Jeff Winter receives a request for information on the Frazier grant from a neighboring farm family, followed by detailed protests on the absence of hearings and environmental review, farmer displacements, water supply motives v. runway protection, price inflation, and the planting of alfalfa and excessive pumping by the Port to the detriment of neighboring wells. In his 5-11-06 response, Winter insists that the purpose of both Olson and Frazier purchases is runway protection, and denies any environmental impact despite admissions by Port executive Kuntz that the Port planted alfalfa for maximum water consumption, and may use the Olson well for Pennbrook.

**05-08-06 FAA says Frazier grant to be conditional on selling unneeded portions, Port protests**
On 5-8-06, the FAA tells the Port the Frazier grant will likely be conditioned on a requirement that both the Frazier and Olson land which is excess to runway protection criteria will need to be sold

by the Port, and the proceeds used to fund another eligible project. Port executive sends angry response. On 5-9-06, the FAA's Winter discusses the portions of the Olson and Frazier land that are unneeded for airport purposes, and cites FAA requirements for sale of unneeded property. Kuntz's response on 5-15-06 further resists resale.

**05-18-06  Citizen group requests outside review of FAA grant actions, receives no response**
On 5-18-06, the Walla Walla 2020 citizens group contacts the FAA about the Port's relationship to the Pennbrook development and requests an outside review of the acquisition and retention proposals by the Port for the Olson and Frazier properties before any further FAA action, as well as copies of all FAA records regarding these properties. On 5-31-06, Regional FAA Administrator Douglas Murphy responds to the request for public records, and promises a separate response to the outside review request. No FAA response on the review request is ever received.

**06-14-06  Citizens group cautions Port on water rights abuse, relinquishment issues**
On 6-14-06, members of the Walla Walla 2020 citizens group discuss with Port executive evidence that the Olson and Frazier water rights have been partially relinquished, and that the Port was planning to unlawfully pump water for alfalfa in excess of the remaining water rights in order to increase its water supply capacity for Pennbrook. Kuntz confirms his intention to pump at the maximum rate, but denies a necessary relationship between these wells and Pennbrook. This denial is repeated in a letter from the Port's attorney to Walla Walla 2020 on 6-26-06.

**07-14-06  FAA awards grant for Frazier purchase without requiring resale of excess lands**
On 7-14-06, the FAA awards the Port a grant of $1,118,095 for the purchase of the entire 262 acre Frazier property, with no resale requirements for the portion of the property that it has determined is unneeded for runway protection. The grant is accepted by the Port on 6-30-06.

**08-03-06*  Citizens group notifies FAA of apparent concealment**
On 8-3-06, the Walla Walla 2020 citizens group notifies the FAA it has evidence of concealment with regard to the grants, which it wants to present to FAA prior to closing and further payment of federal funds. The group also seeks information on environmental compliance, and makes further public record requests to the Port, FAA, and other agencies.

*\*The date indicated in any above entry marked with an asterisk is approximate.*

Each of the documen

# Appendix D: Complaint to Department of Ecology

# WALLA WALLA 2020

September 18, 2006

Bill Neve
Washington State Dept. of Ecology
Walla Walla Office
Walla Walla WA 99362

Re: Port of Walla Walla Olson Well, Certificate #3863-A

Dear Mr. Neve:

We are writing on behalf of the Walla Walla 2020 citizens group, whose members include residents of the City of Walla Walla who depend on the city's municipal water supply, and on behalf of the undersigned holders and users of private water rights in the vicinity of the Port of Walla Walla Olson Well, Permit #3828, Certificate #43863-A issued March 21, 1961.

The undersigned hereby protest the abuse of this certificated water right by its current owner, the Port of Walla Walla, and request that a show cause proceeding be initiated under RCW 90.14.130 and that other action be taken in order to terminate this abuse, and to determine the remaining, unrelinquished extent of the referenced right. RCW 90.14.130 provides that "when it appears" to the Department of Ecology that a water "right has or may have been reverted to the state" because of nonuse, the Department of Ecology *"shall* notify such person by order."

RCW 90.14.180 states, "any person entitled to divert or withdraw waters of the state" who "abandons same, or voluntarily fails, without sufficient cause, to beneficially use all or any part of said right for any period of five successive years *shall* relinquish such right or portion thereof, and such right or portion thereof shall revert to the state." Sufficient cause for nonuse is defined in RCW 90.14.140. As outlined below, the over twenty-year period of partial nonuse of this water right does not meet any of the statutory exceptions to relinquishment.

Our complaint is based on the following facts:

1. Certificate #43863-A was issued on March 21,1961 for 1200 gallons per minute, 1050 acre-feet per year, for irrigation of 300 acres of a 521 acre farm north of the Walla Walla Regional Airport. (Copy of certificate attached)

2. Although sugar beets were grown on a portion of the property in the 1950's through the mid-1970's and apparently utilized the full water right, from the mid-1970's through 1998 the property was primarily devoted to dry land crops, and the capacity and use of the irrigation system was diminished. (See statement of Wayne Knowles, farmer; real estate listing documents with cropping history; Farm Service Agency cropping data; and Pacific Power meter records, attached.)

3. On October 16, 1998, the farm and water right was sold to Keith Olson, a hydrologist with Anderson-Perry engineers. Olson immediately installed a new pump to increase water use, and in 2002 instructed his farm tenant to plant 100 acres of alfalfa in order to justify winter irrigation and to further increase usage. (See attached statement of Wayne Knowles, farmer, and FSA cropping data)

4. In early 2003, Pennbrook Homes of Bend, Oregon began discussions with the Port of Walla Walla regarding the provision of utilities for a major residential development, golf course, and hotel Pennbrook was proposing east of the airport. On March 24, 2004, the Port asked Anderson-Perry and its Walla Walla manager Keith Olson to do a feasibility study. At about that time, Olson proposed the sale of his farm and well to the Port, and instructed his farm tenant to pump 100% of his certificated right during the year 2004, though that exceeded the amount needed for his crops. In July, 2004, Anderson-Perry issued a draft report identifying the Port's need for a new water source to provide 100% of Penn brook's needs, and recommending the Olson well for that purpose. (See attached statement of Wayne Knowles, farmer, and additional documents at www.wallawalla2020.org/chrono/).

5. The Port and Olson entered into purchase negotiations in 2004 and early 2005 centering on the value of the water right, the degree of relinquishment, and the amount that may be transferable to municipal use to serve Pennbrook Homes, which had agreed to contribute to the purchase price. On September 30, 2005, the Port purchased the Olson farm and well with FAA runway protection funds as well as money from Pennbrook. On closing, the Port immediately began implementing plans to increase water consumption from the well by planting 200 additional acres of alfalfa and by installing a new pumping and irrigation system. In November, the final Anderson-Perry report detailed continuing plans to use the well to satisfy all of Pennbrook's needs through the sale of wholesale water by the Port to the developer, which would operate a private water system for the 365 home development, golf course, and hotel. (See documents and additional chronology at www.wallawalla2020.org/chrono/).

6. On June 14,2006, representatives of Walla Walla 2020 met with the Port of Walla Walla director, and discussed evidence of partial relinquishment of the Olson water right and the adjoining water right on the Frazier farm which the Port was in the process of acquiring. The group objected to what it understood to be the Port's plan to unlawfully pump water for 300 acres of alfalfa on the Olson farm in excess of the remaining water right for the property. In response, the Port executive confirmed its intention to pump at the maximum certificated rate for the indefinite future or until such time as an application is made for a transfer to municipal purposes at some undetermined future date. (See attached statement of Bryce Cole, hydrologist).

The pattern of water rights abuse described occurs in the context of a high-profile community focus on questions surrounding the planned Pennbrook development and the importance of protecting the city's adjoining aquifer recharge program, and in the context of an additional apparent course of misconduct by officials of the Port of Walla Walla related to intentional misrepresentation and concealment to obtain federal airport runway protection funds for the purchase of the Olson and Frazier properties, documentation of which is also available at www.wallawalla2020.org/chrono/. See a copy of the letter of complaint to the FAA, which is conducting its own investigation, at http://ww2020.bmi.netipennbrook.%20faa%20letter.%208-2l-06.doc.

The abuse described affects the interests of users of the City of Walla Walla municipal water supply and the users and holders of private water rights in the vicinity. The undersigned are aggrieved by it, and therefore request that a show cause proceeding be initiated under RCW 90.14.130 and that other measures be taken to terminate the abuse, and to determine the remaining, unrelinquished extent of Certificate #3863-A.

We look forward to the acknowledgement of our request, and notice of the steps the Department will be taking in response.

Sincerely,

Daniel N. Clark
Project Coordinator
Walla Walla 2020
clarkdn@charter.net

Michael Ponti
740 Sapolil East Road
Walla Walla W A 99362
Certificate # ____

Kathleen S. Ponti
740 Sapolil East Road
Walla Walla W A 99362
Certificate # _____

James S. Robison
2839 Robison Ranch Rd.
Walla Walla W A 99362
Certificate # _____
Certificate # _____

Jane M. Robison
2839 Robison Ranch Rd.
Walla Walla WA 99362
Certificate # _____
Certificate # _____

Susan Robison Kummer
2788 Robison Ranch Rd.
Walla Walla WA 99362
Certificate #_____
Certificate #_____

Darrell Dean Angell
3686 Lower Waitsburg Rd.
Walla Walla WA 99362
Certificate #G320591C

Carol Ann Angell
3686 Lower Waitsburg Rd.
Walla Walla W A 99362
Certificate #G320591C

James L. Angell
3132 Arrowhead Rd
Cheyenne, WY
Certificate # G320591C

# STATEMENT OF WAYNE KNOWLES

My name is Kenneth Wayne Knowles. I reside at 1257 Valley Chapel Road, Walla Walla, Washington, and do business as Knowles Farms, Inc. My family and then my cousin and I farmed the Moore/Olson land northeast of the Walla Walla airport for over 40 years, beginning in the 1950's, and ending in 2005.

During that time we raised mostly wheat, barley, dry and green peas, garbanzos, and some canola. When my family first moved onto the farm, the irrigation pump was new and we had enough water to pump 200 sprinklers. We raised sugar beets on part of the property in the 50's, 60's, and early 70's, which used the maximum water right. Toward the end of the beet growing in the valley, the condition of the pump deteriorated, and the maximum we could pump was 120 sprinklers, even with a booster pump.

I have looked over the 10-year cropping history in the attached listing documents prepared by Coldwell Banker for the Elsie Moore Grandchildren Trust in 1998 when the farm was put up for sale, as well as the attached cropping records from the Farm Service Agency, and they appear generally accurate as to our cropping during that period.

When Keith Olson bought the farm in the fall of 1998, he continued to lease it to me. One of the first things Keith did after buying the property was to put in a new pump, so he could increase water use. In 2002, Keith also had us put in 100 acres of alfalfa so we could water during the winter and further increase usage.

In 2004, Keith told me to pump 100% of the certificated right. Even though water rates are cheaper during the irrigation season from April to October, Keith told me to keep pumping past the season into November and December when the rates are higher. After wheat, we watered the stubble, then back to the alfalfa after the last cutting. We ran 48 hour sets just to use as much water as we could. The only way to use the full right was to pump it when you didn't need it.

Before Keith sold the property to the Port, he terminated our farm lease, which was a condition required by the Port.

Dated this 15th day of August, 2006.


_____(signed)_____
K. Wayne Knowles

# STATEMENT OF BRYCE COLE

My name is Bryce Cole. I reside at 708 SE 4th, College Place, Washington. I am an engineering professor at Walla Walla College.

On June 14, 2006, I participated in a meeting at the Port of Walla Walla offices in Walla Walla with Port executive director Jim Kuntz, Ralph Gregory of Pennbrook Homes, my father Jon Cole who is also an engineering professor at Walla Walla College, and Daniel Clark of Walla Walla 2020.

During the meeting, Mr. Clark brought up the subject of the Port's plan to supply water to Pennbrook's proposed development adjacent to the airport, to which Mr. Kuntz responded that he didn't understand the problem. Mr. Clark then mentioned the competing demands for water in the deep aquifer between the City of Walla Walla and the Port. He also mentioned his understanding that the Port intended to pump the full certificated water right from the recently acquired Olson/Moore well for alfalfa the Port was planting, despite the partial relinquishment of water rights on both the Olson well and the Frazier well that the Port was in the process of acquiring, because prior owners had not put the full amount of their rights to beneficial use over the years, as demonstrated by Farm Service Agency crop records showing planting of lower water use crops for many years.

Mr. Kuntz denied there had been any relinquishment of the rights for these wells, and declared that the Port will pump the full amount of the certificated right until such time as it applies for a transfer of the certificate to municipal purposes at some undetermined time in the future. He further stated that Mr. Clark was mistaken in concluding that these wells would be used for the Pennbrook project. Mr. Clark stated that continuing to pump water that had clearly been relinquished would be harmful to the public and neighboring users, and would be unlawful, and that if the Port insisted on doing that, his organization would try to stop them. Mr. Kuntz then left the room, and the meeting ended.

Dated this 16th day of August, 2006.

_____(signed)_____
Bryce Cole

# Appendix E, Brief of Appellant,
# Walla Walla 2020 v. W.W. County & Pennbrook Homes, Inc.

**IN THE SUPERIOR COURT FOR THE COUNTY OF WALLA WALLA
IN AND FOR THE STATE OF WASHINGTON**

| | |
|---|---|
| WALLA WALLA 2020, a<br>Washington nonprofit corporation,<br>                  Petitioner<br>        vs.<br>WALLA WALLA COUNTY,<br>PENNBROOK HOMES, INC., and<br>CITIZENS FOR GOOD GOVERNANCE<br>        Respondents | No. 06-2-00974-7<br><br><br>**BRIEF OF APPELLANT** |

## TABLE OF CONTENTS

## I. INTRODUCTION

Appellant Walla Walla 2020 is a citizens group made up of a cross-section of people deeply concerned about the community.  The group has been involved in land use and other quality of life issues in the Walla Walla Valley since 1988.

The essential issues involved in this case are whether Walla Walla County complied with the State Environmental Policy Act, RCW Ch. 43.21C (SEPA) and with its own procedures when it processed an application for Illahee, the largest development in Walla Walla's history. Walla Walla 2020 is appealing the failure of Walla Walla County to require an environmental impact statement for  Illahee.  Instead of requiring the comprehensive environmental analysis contemplated by SEPA, the County authorized this significant project to proceed on the basis of a Mitigated Determination of Non-Significance, which fails to give due consideration to the proposal's impacts on water, water utilities, environmental health, air and ground transportation, and community housing needs.

## II. PROCEDURAL AND FACTUAL SUMMARY

In August 2003, Pennbrook Homes, a Bend, Oregon developer, identified several hundred acres of prime farmland leading to the foothills of the Blue Mountains east of Walla Walla as a site for the community's first destination resort (Vol. 4, Bk. 2, I, p.2). In October, 2003, Pennbrook and the owner of the property approached the City of Walla Walla with a proposal to develop the site, which was outside the city's Urban Growth Area (UGA) east of the Walla Walla Regional Airport. An application was filed to expand the UGA to include the proposed site by amending the Urban Area Comprehensive Plan. (Vol. 6, A-8, note 4)

In December 2003, in response to notice of the application and after preliminary discussions with the developer, the Port of Walla Walla wrote to the City to express its concern about "allowing housing and other non-compatible land uses to surround the airport," declaring,

> One of our central concerns is that the Port cannot predict the type, size, and frequency of aircraft that may be using our airport 5 to 10 years from now. It very well could be a mix of private, commercial and military aircraft. Some of these aircraft could cause a land use conflict in the proposed revised urban growth boundary. This could be especially true for aircraft flying an approach into runway 25 or taking off on runway 07. Both scenarios would have aircraft flying low over the proposed revised urban growth boundary.

The Port further wrote,

> The Walla Walla Regional Airport Industrial Park is immediately east of the proposed revision (sic) urban growth boundary and is only separated by U.S. Highway 12. The Port anticipates the industrial park to grow substantially over the next 10 to 20 years …Any development which incorporates residential housing near U.S. Highway 12 is of concern. Two large agribusinesses are located up wind from this proposed area. While both have outstanding environmental records, the very nature of their business causes at times smells and release of products into the atmosphere" (Vol. 6, A-8, note 5).

Subsequently, in March 2004, the Port and Pennbrook began discussions about how the Port could supply water to the development as a revenue source to the Port. In connection with those negotiations, the Port advised the developer against annexing to the City (Vol.6, A-8, n 6).

They then arranged with the Anderson-Perry engineering firm for a study of the Port's capacity to supply water to the project. After the Port notified local governments of the study, the

City expressed concerns about the effect groundwater withdrawals for the project by the Port would have on the City's deep aquifer recharge program, and requested that the study also look at the potential for city water to be supplied to the development from the City's combined surface and ground water supplies (Vol. 6, A-8, n.11-12, 18).

In July 2004, Anderson-Perry issued a report concluding that the Port needed an additional water source to supply Pennbrook. Interestingly, the report focused on the adjoining farm owned by Keith Olson, the Anderson-Perry manager and engineer who initially worked on the study. Olson proposed to sell his farm and deep aquifer well to the Port for this purpose (Vol. 6, A-8, n.13, 9). Pennbrook agreed to assist the Port in buying the Olson property for this purpose with FAA runway protection funds, though the Port concealed this relationship from the FAA (Vol. 6, A-8, note 14, 16, 19-23).

In August 2004, notwithstanding its earlier protests, the Port drafted, submitted, and began lobbying the County and City to change comprehensive plan policies to eliminate prohibitions against housing encroachment in the vicinity of the airport, and to permit it to be the water supplier for nearby residential development (Vol. 6, A-8, n.15).

On October 31, 2005, the Walla Walla county commissioners approved a variety of changes to the Walla Walla Urban Area Comprehensive Plan sought by Pennbrook and the Port, putting the project site into the UGA, and adding an Urban Planned Communities (UPC) chapter to the county zoning code (Vol. 8, P-10, Ord. 322). Citizens for Good Governance appealed those non-project actions to the Growth Management Hearings Board for Eastern Washington. The Port of Walla Walla intervened in the action to protect its new water utility venture. The appeal was rejected (Vol. 8, P-11).

Pennbrook filed the present development application in December, 2005 as an Urban Planned Community of 365 single-family homes, a nine-hole golf course, hotel, restaurant, and related commercial facilities on 358 acres, south and east of Highway 12, west of Harbert Road and north of the City's water treatment plant. The applicant filed an accompanying environmental checklist to attempt to satisfy SEPA requirements for the proposed development, which adjoins the city's water treatment plant. The checklist specifies that water will be provided by the Port of Walla Walla, and that no ground water will be withdrawn for the project (Vol. 4, Bk. 2, B, pp. 3, 6, 15). The checklist further states that there are no off-site sources of emissions that may affect the proposal, and no environmental health hazards including potential exposure to toxic chemicals. Again, despite the Port's earlier warnings, the checklist does not mention the immediately adjacent toxic chemical facilities (Ibid, pp. 5, 9). Regarding the number of high, middle, and low-income housing units to be provided and proposed measures to reduce housing impacts, the checklist states there are no significant housing impacts, and that a range of income types will be provided (Ibid, p.11-12). No mention or analysis of air transportation conflicts with the adjacent general aviation airport is provided in the checklist (Ibid, p. 14).

On June 16, 2006, the director of the Walla Walla County Community Development Department issued a Mitigated Determination of Non-Significance for the project. The MDNS was appealed under the county code by Walla Walla 2020 and Citizens for Good Governance on the basis of water, environmental health, housing, transportation, and utilities impacts (Vol. 3, 14; Vol. 2, 1-2).

On October 3, Walla Walla County hearing examiner LeAnna Toweill heard the appeal as provided by the county code. The hearing examiner conducted a separate hearing the same day on the UPC master plan and development application on referral by the county commissioners. On October 25, the hearing examiner issued consolidated Findings, Conclusions, and Recommendations that the SEPA appeals be denied and that the UPC master plan and development agreement be approved with minor modifications (Vol. 1, 3).

The county commissioners immediately scheduled the matter for action, and on October 27, petitioner filed a Motion to Strike the matter from the commissioners' October 30th calendar, giving notice to the Board of its intention to file a Motion for Reconsideration with the Hearing Examiner pursuant to the Hearing Examiner Rules of Procedure. On October 30, the Board of Commissioners ruled that the hearing examiner had no jurisdiction to hear a Motion for Reconsideration, having only issued a recommendation rather than a final decision.

Walla Walla 2020 then filed a Motion for Ruling on Jurisdiction with the hearing examiner, and on November 2, 2006 the hearing examiner ruled that she lacked further jurisdiction (Vol 2, 19; Vol. 1, 4). On November 13, the Board of Commissioners adopted resolution 06-324 concurring with the Findings and Conclusion of the hearing examiner, denying the SEPA appeals and approving the proposed UPC master plan and development agreement with modifications (Vol. 1,1).

The petitioner appeals these decisions on both substantive and procedural grounds.

## III. ISSUES

1. Did the hearing examiner and the board of commissioners engage in unlawful procedure and fail to follow prescribed processes when they failed to allow petitioner to file a motion for reconsideration, as expressly authorized by the county code?

2. Was the action of the board of commissioners beyond its authority when it issued a final decision on petitioner's SEPA appeal, a matter exclusively within the hearing examiner's jurisdiction?

3. Did the appellant sufficiently demonstrate the inadequacy of the county's SEPA determination by its failure to properly consider and mitigate the project's impact on groundwater and public water supplies?

4. Did the appellant sufficiently demonstrate the inadequacy of the county's SEPA determination by neglecting to consider the project's failure to comply with numerous state and local water resource plans and policies?

5. Did the appellant sufficiently demonstrate the inadequacy of the county's SEPA determination by its failure to consider and mitigate the project's impact on environmental health due to potential toxic chemical releases?

6. Did the appellant sufficiently demonstrate the inadequacy of the county's SEPA determination by its failure to properly consider and mitigate the project's impact on housing?

7. Did the appellant sufficiently demonstrate the inadequacy of the county's SEPA determination by its failure to consider and mitigate the project's impacts relating to air and ground transportation?

8. Did the appellant sufficiently demonstrate the inadequacy of the county's SEPA determination by its failure to consider and mitigate the project's impact on utilities?

9. Did the appellant sufficiently demonstrate the inadequacy of the county's SEPA determination by its failure to properly Consider and mitigate the project's cumulative impacts on groundwater and public water supplies, its conflicts with state and local water resource plans and policies, and its impacts relating to environmental health, housing, transportation, and utilities?

10. Was it clear error for the county to issue an MDNS under SEPA when the evidence demonstrates significant adverse impacts on groundwater and public water supplies,

environmental health, housing, transportation, utilities, and the project's conflicts with state and local plans and policies?

# IV. ARGUMENT

## A. STANDARD OF REVIEW

### 1. Land Use Petition Act Standards

RCW 36.70C.130(1) provides the following standards for review under LUPA:

The court may grant relief only if the party seeking relief has carried the burden of establishing that one of the standards set forth in (a) through (f) of this subsection has been met. The standards are:

(a) The body or officer that made the land use decision engaged in unlawful procedure or failed to follow a prescribed process, unless the error was harmless;

(b) The land use decision is an erroneous interpretation of the law, after allowing for such deference as is due the construction of a law by a local jurisdiction with expertise;

(c) The land use decision is not supported by evidence that is substantial when viewed in light of the whole record before the court;

(d) The land use decision is a clearly erroneous application of the law to the facts;

(e) The land use decision is outside the authority or jurisdiction of the body or officer making the decision; or

(f) The land use decision violates the constitutional rights of the party seeking relief.

An agency action is clearly erroneous if "the reviewing court on the record is left with a definite and firm conviction that a mistake has been committed." Anderson v. Pierce County, 86 Wn. App. 290, 301, 936 P.2d 432 (1997). The court need not find local government action to be arbitrary and capricious, RCW 36.70C.130(2), though action found to be arbitrary, capricious or an abuse of discretion would be contrary to law and would require invalidation. See *Pierce County Sheriff v. Civil Serv. Comm'n,* 98 Wn.2d 690, 693-94, 658 P.2d 648 (1983). (An agency's violation of rules that govern its exercise of discretion is considered contrary to law and amounts to arbitrary and capricious action.)

The procedural issues presented in this appeal are reviewable *de novo* as involving questions of the construction of law. RCW 36.70C.130(1)(a)(b)(d)&(e). Construction of an ordinance, like a statute, presents a question of law and is reviewed *de novo*. *Faben Point Neighbors v. City of Mercer Island*, 102 Wn.App. 775, 778, 11 P.3d 322, *review denied*, 142 Wn.2d 1027, 21 P.3d 1149 (2000), citing *McTavish v. City of Bellevue*, 89 Wn. App. 561, 564, 949 P.2d 837 (1998). Likewise, whether land use decisions satisfy requirements of law also presents a question of law and is reviewable *de novo*. *Sunderland Family Treatment Services v. City of Pasco,* 107 Wn. App. 109, 117, 26 P.3d 955 (2001) ("Issues of law are reviewed de novo.") and *United Development Corp. v. City of Mill Creek* 106 Wn. App. 681, 687-688, 26 P.3d 943 (2001) ("Factual findings are considered under the substantial evidence standard and conclusions of law are reviewed de novo.").

## 2. State Environmental Policy Act Standards

### a. SEPA Is To Be Given Broad And Vigorous Enforcement.

The State Environmental Policy Act contains both procedural requirements and substantive authority. Procedurally, the statute requires the integrated use of environmental values in decision making by all state and local agencies. RCW 43.21C.030(2)(a). Substantively, SEPA grants governmental agencies the authority to use the environmental documentation to condition, and even deny, specific projects and other governmental actions based upon environmental impacts. RCW 43.21C.060.

An environmental impact statement is required to be prepared for all major actions that significantly affect the quality of the environment. RCW 43.21C.030(2)(c). Because complete and accurate information is a prerequisite to sound environmental action, the requirements of SEPA have been construed liberally.

In one of its earliest decisions on SEPA, the Washington Supreme Court declared unequivocally that SEPA is to be given "broad and vigorous construction." *Eastlake Community Council v. Roanoke Associates, Inc.*, 82 Wn.2d 475, 490, 513 P.2d 46 (1973). As the court noted in the often-cited language from *Eastlake*, 82 Wn. 2d at 490:

> To fulfill these purposes of restoring ecological health to our lives, SEPA <u>mandates</u> governmental bodies to consider the total environmental and ecological factors to the fullest in deciding major matters. The procedural duties imposed by SEPA - - full consideration to environmental protection - - are to be exercised to the fullest extent possible to insure that the "attempt by the people to shape their future environment by

deliberation, not default" will be realized.  *Stempel v. Department of Water Resources, supra*, 82 Wash.2d at 118, 508 P.2d at 172.

**b. An MDNS Must Be Based On Consideration Of All Environmental Factors.**

In rendering a threshold determination, the County was required to "[d]etermine if the proposal is likely to have a probable significant adverse environmental impact . . ." WAC 197-11-330(1)(b).  The term "significant" is construed in WAC197-11-797:

> 1) "Significant" as used in SEPA means a reasonable likelihood of more than a moderate adverse impact on environmental quality.
> (2) Significance involves context and intensity (WAC <u>197-11-330</u>) and does not lend itself to a formula or quantifiable test. The context may vary with the physical setting. Intensity depends on the magnitude and duration of an impact.

The severity of an impact should be weighed along with the likelihood of its occurrence. An impact may be significant if its chance of occurrence is not great, but the resulting environmental impact would be severe if it occurred. WAC 197-11-797(3).

In reaching this determination, the record must reflect "actual consideration of environmental factors." *Norway Hill Preservation and Protection Association v. King County Council*, 87 Wn.2d 267, 275, 552 P.2d 674 (1976).  The decision record upon which the environmental determination is based must demonstrate the agency actually weighed the environmental impacts of the proposed action:

> The SEPA policies of full disclosure and consideration of environmental values require actual consideration of environmental factors before a determination of no environmental significance can be made. . . . As a result, a reviewing court will always have a complete record upon which to review a 'negative threshold determination.'

> In the absence of a record sufficient 'to demonstrate that environmental factors were considered in a manner sufficient to amount to prima facie compliance with the procedural requirements of SEPA,' . . . a 'negative threshold determination' could not be sustained upon review even under the 'arbitrary or capricious' standard because the determination would lack sufficient support in the record.

87 Wn. 2d at 274.  Even though *Norway Hill* is one of the earliest decisions under SEPA, its holdings continue to be followed in more recent SEPA cases.  In *Wenatchee Sportsmen Ass'n v.*

*Chelan County*, 141 Wn.2d 169, 172, 4 P.3d 123 (2000) the court re-affirmed the closer scrutiny of SEPA threshold decisions:

> For the MDNS to survive judicial scrutiny, the record must demonstrate that environmental factors were considered in a manner sufficient to amount to prima facie compliance with the procedural requirements of SEPA and that the decision to issue an MDNS was based on information sufficient to evaluate the proposal's environmental impact.

A threshold determination is based upon the applicant's completion of an environmental checklist, "which must provide information reasonably sufficient to evaluate the environmental impact of the proposal." *Anderson v. Pierce County*, 86 Wn. App. 290, 301 (1997); WAC 197-11-315-335.

### c.    An MDNS Must Be Based Upon A Consideration Of Alternatives.

Consideration of alternatives is required at the threshold determination level.  In pertinent part, SEPA provides in RCW 43.21C.030(2):

> all branches of government of this state, including state agencies, municipal and public corporations and counties shall:  . . . (e) Study, develop, and describe appropriate alternatives to recommended courses of action in any proposal which involves unresolved conflicts concerning alternative uses of available resources.

See *Yakama Indian Nation v. State Department of Ecology*, PCHB No. 93-157, *et al.* in which the Board construed RCW 43.21C.030(2)(e) to stand independent of SEPA's directive to consider alternatives in the EIS process under subsection 43.21C.030(2)(c)(iii).

The Department of Ecology regulations that implement SEPA underscore the need to discuss alternatives in order to facilitate reasoned decision-making by government officials and the public.  "Proposals should be described in ways that encourage considering and comparing alternatives," WAC 197-11-060(3)(a)(iii).


## B. THE HEARING EXAMINER AND THE BOARD OF COMMISSIONERS ENGAGED IN UNLAWFUL PROCEDURE AND FAILED TO FOLLOW PRESCRIBED PROCESSES.  THE DECISION OF THE BOARD OF COMMISSIONERS WAS BEYOND ITS AUTHORITY.

*The hearing examiner engaged in unlawful procedure and failed to follow prescribed processes under RCW 36.70C.130(1)(a) in failing to issue a final decision on the SEPA appeal and in refusing to hear appellant's motion for reconsideration. The county commissioners engaged in unlawful procedure and failed to follow prescribed processes in refusing to allow the hearing examiner to hear a motion for reconsideration. The commissioners' issuance of a final decision on the SEPA appeal was beyond their authority under RCW 36.70C.130(1)(e).*

Under the Walla Walla County Code, appeals of threshold determinations under SEPA are to be heard and decided by a county hearing examiner. WWCC 14.11.010 provides in part that "appeals of administrative decisions or determinations made pursuant to RCW 43.21C may be appealed, by applicants or parties of record, to the hearing examiner…" WWCC 14.03.050 provides that "The hearing examiner shall review and make decisions on the following applications: …(J) Appeals alleging an error in administrative decisions or determinations pursuant to Chapter 43.21C RCW…."

WWCC 14.11.020 provides,

### 14.11.020 Appeal of hearing examiner decisions.
Appeals of a rezone not of general applicability (site-specific) shall be made to the board of county commissioners for review at a closed record appeal as provided for in Section 14.11.030 of this chapter. <u>All other decisions of the hearing examiner may be appealed, by applicants or parties of record from the hearing examiner public hearing to the Walla Walla County Superior Court</u> as provided for in Section 14.11.040 of this chapter; provided, however, that <u>no final decision of the hearing examiner may be appealed to Walla Walla County Superior Court unless such party has first brought a timely motion for reconsideration of the hearing examiner's decision pursuant to Section 14.11.060 of this chapter</u> (emphasis added).

WWCC 14.11.060 provides for reconsideration as follows:

An applicant or party of record to a hearing examiner's public hearing may seek reconsideration only of a final decision by filing a written request for reconsideration with the administrator within ten days of the final decision. The request shall comply with WWCC Section 14.11.030(B). The hearing examiner shall, within thirty days of receipt of the request for reconsideration, consider the request at a public meeting, without public comment or argument by the party filing the request. If the request is denied, the previous action shall become final. If the request is granted, the hearing examiner may immediately revise and reissue its decision or may call for argument in accordance with the procedures for closed record appeals. Reconsideration will be granted only when an obvious legal error has occurred or a material factual issue has been overlooked that would change the previous decision.

In addition, Rule 11.3.c of the Walla Walla County Land Use Hearing Examiner Rules of Procedure and Appeals provides,

1) Any party of record may file a written request with the Hearing

Examiner for reconsideration of a final decision within ten calendar days of the date of the Hearing Examiner's decision. ...

2) The Hearing Examiner shall respond to the request for reconsideration within ten days by issuing an Order on Reconsideration. The Order on Reconsideration may:

a) deny the request for reconsideration;
b) approve the request by modifying or amending the initial final decision based on the established record;
c) approve the request based on additional evidence added to the established record upon a showing of significant relevance and good cause for delay in its submission, consistent with Rule 9.8(g); or,
d) set the matter for additional public hearing.

Rule 9.8(g) provides

Submission of additional evidence after close of record. After the close of the record in a given matter, additional evidence may only be submitted upon a Request for Reconsideration based on new evidence not available at the time of the public hearing. Additional evidence will only be considered upon a showing of significant relevance and good cause for delay in its submission. All parties of record will be given notice of the consideration of such evidence and granted an opportunity to review such evidence and submit rebuttal arguments.

The hearing examiner on November 2 refused to entertain a motion for reconsideration based on the fact that she had not issued a final decision, only a recommendation. Yet such a decision was required of her by WWCC 14.11.10 and 14.03.50. Prior to her refusal, the board of commissioners had also ruled that she had no authority to entertain such a motion. Rather than allowing the hearing examiner to decide the matter, the board of commissioners then itself made the decision. This was beyond their authority on land use matters, which is limited to actions on recommendations of the planning commission, final plat approvals, and appeals of certain rezones as provided in WWCC 14.03.030.

The responsibility of the hearing examiner to decide rather than merely recommend is neither delegable nor insubstantial. The right under the rules and ordinance to move for reconsideration of a dispositive ruling is also a substantial right, including in this instance the right to seek admission of new evidence not available at the time of the hearing. In this case, such evidence includes the findings of the Federal Aviation Administration (FAA) resulting from its investigation of the Port of Walla Walla/Pennbrook relationship, which were issued on October 27, 2006, after the close of the hearing record in this matter and within the time for filing a motion for reconsideration of the October 25 issuance of the hearing examiner's recommendations. Those findings are based in large part on the nearly 400 pages of documentation presented by appellant which are part of the record on this appeal at Vol. 6, A-8.

A key conclusion of the 71-page FAA findings, excerpts from which are appended hereto as Attachment A, is that the Port of Walla Walla intentionally misrepresented or concealed the objective, benefits, and parties involved in its application for federal funds to purchase the 521 acre Olson farm and deep aquifer well, with knowledge of the falsity of its misrepresentations, and with the intention that the FAA rely on those misrepresentations to its detriment. Those findings specifically concluded that a major objective of the Olson acquisition "was the need for Pennbrook to obtain water for its development and the Port's desire to provide water as a revenue source." (p. 9). The findings detail that,

> Four months prior to discussing the Olson property purchase with the FAA, the Port entered into numerous conversations with Pennbrook regarding the supply of water. During this time the Port received an initial assessment that the Port's current water supply was not sufficient to support Pennbrook. Prior to submitting its grant application, (the) Port entered into negotiations with Pennbrook to accept $422,175 for the purchase of the Olson farm in consideration of supplying water.

> Meanwhile, the Port presented to the FAA numerous justifications for the purchase including RPZ, MANPADS, 50:1 transitional zone, and uneconomic remnants. On four occasions during the application period there was an opportunity to provide the FAA with an accurate representation of the Port's interest in supplying water...

> The Port never informed the FAA of its pending agreement with Pennbrook to accept payment with the condition of supplying water. Instead, the Port continued to mislead the FAA that the primary use of the water was for the industrial park. (pp. 9-10)

The actions related to this project that are described in these findings are defined as criminal behavior under 18 USC 1001.

Additional evidence of unlawful activity associated with the Port's agreement with the applicant to supply water to this development also became available after the time the hearing record was closed on October 5 and within the time for reconsideration. Appended to this brief as Attachment B is the October 16, 2006 letter of warning from the Department of Ecology to the

Port of Walla Walla responding to the September 22 letter of complaint from appellant which is in the record at Vol. 6, A10 (see Attachment C), addressing the apparent over-pumping of the Olson water right by the Port in preparation for a future transfer application in order to serve this project. Further evidence of such unlawful pumping by the Port as the proposed supplier for this development has also arisen since the close of the record, and should be addressed on a motion for reconsideration.

Evidence of misconduct associated with water issues related to the water provider proposed by respondent Pennbrook to draw water for this project from the aquifer block serving the Walla Walla urban area further indicates the potentially significant adverse impacts of the respondent's water supply plans, and merits serious consideration by the hearing officer before issuing a final decision in this matter.

The hearing examiner and the board of commissioners have failed to follow prescribed processes and have engaged in unlawful procedures with respect to both reconsideration and the issuance of a final decision on the SEPA appeal. In addition, the board of commissioners rendered a final decision on the SEPA appeal beyond their lawful authority. Their decision approving the UPC application prior to a final decision on the SEPA appeal was also unlawful under WAC 197-11-310.

The matter should be remanded to the hearing officer under RCW 36.70C.130(1)(a) and (e) for further proceedings consistent with the county code and rules of procedure.

## C. THE APPELLANT HAS MET ITS BURDEN OF PROOF WITH RESPECT TO WATER IMPACTS

*Conclusions I.F.1-I.F.6 are an erroneous interpretation of the law and a clearly erroneous application of the law to the facts under RCW 36.70C.130(b) and (d).*

Respondent Pennbrook's proposal for water supply to the project from the Port of Walla Walla to a new private water system is in serious conflict with state and local water policies. No sufficient analysis has been made of the impacts of the proposal on groundwater and public water systems, or of supply alternatives, and no mitigation of probable adverse impacts has been required.

Groundwater movement, quantity and quality, and public water supplies are elements of the environment which must be considered in any environmental analysis. WAC 197-11-444(1)(c)(iv-v).

The 358 acre project site is currently a dryland farm (Vol. 5, #1, p.12). All water for the proposed 365 homes, nine-hole golf course, 65-unit hotel, and commercial complex including restaurant and other commercial uses is proposed to be supplied exclusively from groundwater, utilizing a new, privately operated water system to be established by respondent Pennbrook to serve this project with water wholesaled from the Port of Walla Walla's basalt aquifer wells (Finding 83-86).

The Port's wells draw from the same deep aquifer as City of Walla Walla Wells #1, 2, and 3 (Findings 98-100), an aquifer that had been experiencing steady declines for decades leading up to reduced pumping and the initiation of a recharge program by the City (Finding 103). The City obtains approximately 87% of the water for its public supply system from surface rights in Mill Creek, but relies on the deep aquifer for its remaining 13%, particularly during times of low flow in the summer or excessive turbidity in the winter. In addition, a fire in the City's watershed could require the City to rely wholly on ground water for several years (Vol.6, A-15, pp. 1-1, 1-17).

As a result of the declines in the aquifer and other factors, the City has made substantial investment in an Aquifer Storage and Recovery (ARS) program to inject treated Mill Creek water into the basalt aquifer during high flows through its Well #1, located a few hundred yards from the Port's primary Well #1. With implementation of the recharge program and under present use rates, the decline of the aquifer has been halted (Vol. 8, P-5, p.21).

Under WAC 197-11-330(3), "In determining an impact's significance, the responsible official shall take into account that…(e) A proposal may to a significant degree…(iii) Conflict with local, state, or federal laws or requirements for the protection of the environment…(emphasis added)"

## 1. *The Proposed Project is Contrary to Washington State Water Policy*

Allowing Illahee to be served through an expansion of the Port's water system and the creation of a new, private water system by Pennbrook contravenes state water policy.

Washington State water policies are set out in the Water Resources Act, RCW Chapter 90.54, which declares in RCW 90.54.010:

> (1) The legislature finds that:
> (a) Proper utilization of the water resources of this state is necessary to the promotion of public health and the economic well-being of the state and the preservation of its natural resources and aesthetic values. Although water is a renewable resource, its supply and availability are becoming increasingly limited, particularly during summer and fall months and dry years when demand is greatest....
> (2) It is the purpose of this chapter to set forth fundamentals of water resource policy for the state to insure that waters of the state are protected and fully utilized for the greatest benefit to the people of the state of Washington and, in relation thereto, to provide direction to the department of ecology, other state agencies and officials, and local government in carrying out water and related resources programs.

RCW 90.54.020 provides:

> Utilization and management of the waters of the state shall be guided by the following general declaration of fundamentals....
>
> (8) Development of water supply systems, whether publicly or privately owned, which provide water to the public generally in regional areas within the state shall be encouraged. *Development of water supply systems for multiple domestic use which will not serve the public generally shall be discouraged where water supplies are available from water systems serving the public.* (emphasis added)

In addition to SEPA, state law provides cities and counties the power to implement this policy by requiring connection to an existing public water supply system:

> ...In addition to other authorities, the county or city may impose conditions on building permits requiring connection to an existing public water system where the existing system is willing and able to provide safe and reliable potable water to the applicant with reasonable economy and efficiency. RCW 19.27.097(1)

In order to provide Walla Walla County with sufficient information on the environmental consequences of failing to implement this state water policy in the case of respondent Pennbrook's large development, an environmental impact statement should be required, including consideration of alternative sources of supply,.

Under WAC 197-11-055, the environmental impacts of this and other project actions should be considered at the beginning of the project, rather than in a piecemeal fashion such as at later platting and building permit stages.

(1) The SEPA process shall be integrated with agency activities at the earliest possible time to ensure that planning and decisions reflect environmental values, to avoid delays later in the process, and to seek to resolve potential problems.

(2) The lead agency shall prepare its threshold determination and environmental impact statement (EIS), if required, at the earliest possible point in the planning and decision-making process, when the principal features of a proposal and its environmental impacts can be reasonably identified.
(a) A proposal exists when an agency is presented with an application or has a goal and is actively preparing to make a decision on one or more alternative means of accomplishing that goal *and* the environmental effects can be meaningfully evaluated.
(i) The fact that proposals may require future agency approvals or environmental review shall not preclude current consideration, as long as proposed future activities are specific enough to allow some evaluation of their environmental impacts.

Throughout this case, respondent Pennbrook has made clear that intends to obtain water for the project from the Port of Walla Walla. Therefore, this feature is clearly defined, and the environmental analysis should take place now.

Conclusion 1.F.1 and 1.F.6 that appellants have not met their burden of proof because water issues can be determined at a later time are an erroneous interpretation of the law and a clearly erroneous application of the law to the facts under RCW 36.70C.103(1)(b) and (d).

## 2. *The Proposed Project Contravenes the Walla Walla/College Place Coordinated Water System Plan*

The County's approval of an arrangement that supplies the Illahee development exclusively from groundwater provided by the Port of Walla Walla conflicts with multiple policies of the Walla Walla/College Place Coordinated Water System Plan.

Pursuant to the Public Water System Coordination Act, RCW Chapter 70.116, in 1982, the Walla Walla-College Place Urban Area was declared a Critical Water Supply Area (Vol. 6, A-16, pp.I-2, I-3).

"Critical water supply service area" means a geographical area which is characterized by a proliferation of small, inadequate water systems, or by water supply problems which threaten the present or future water quality or reliability of service in such a manner that efficient and orderly development may best be achieved through coordinated planning by the water utilities in the area. RCW 70.116.30(2)

Under the provisions of RCW 70.116.040(1),

> ....After establishment of the external boundaries of the critical water supply service area, no new public water systems may be approved within the boundary area unless an existing water purveyor is unable to provide water service.

Pursuant to the Act, a Coordinated Water System Plan (CWSP) was adopted by the Walla Walla County Commissioners in March, 1984 for the Walla Walla/College Place Critical Water Supply Service Area (CWSSA), which includes the project site. An update of the initial plan was completed in October, 1994. (Vol. 6, A-16, A-17, pp. II-1, III-10)        Those who participated in the planning process for the update included the City of Walla Walla, the Walla Walla Airport administered by the Port of Walla Walla, respondent Walla Walla County, and appellant Walla Walla 2020, among others (Vol. 6, A-17, p. ii).

One of the stated goals of the updated CWSP plan was:

> --Establishing future water service areas and a procedure for approving the water system requirements for new development. (Vol. 6, A-17, p. II-2)

To accomplish this, each utility was requested to identify its existing and future service areas.

No plan to expand the Port of Walla Walla's airport service area beyond the boundaries of the airport was included in the original plan or the 1994 Update. (Vol. 6, A-17, pp. VI-5, III-15) By contrast, the City of Walla Walla's service area boundary was expanded in the Update to include the Urban Growth Boundaries established under the Growth Management Act. Under the plan's provisions,

> Walla Walla County (County) is to refer new developments requiring public water supply to existing, expanding utilities as a first step in obtaining water service. If the proposed development is within the designated service area of an expanding system, it is intended that the system serve the development. If the proposed development is outside of designated service areas, adjacent systems authorized to expand are to be given the first opportunity for service. *The goal of this process is to minimize the creation of new public water systems.* (Vol. 6, A-17, p.VIII-1, emphasis added)

In addition to designating the City of Walla Walla as the service provider for the UGA, the City of Walla Walla was designated in the plan as the exclusive Satellite System Agency (SMA) with responsibility:

> To provide water service to new developments located within that portion of the CWSSA not designated as the service area of existing utilities. (Vol. 6, A-177, pp. II-3,4)

In the 1984 CWSP, the Walla Walla County Engineering Department had been designated as the satellite service agency. The operating provisions included the following arrangements for new developments outside designated service areas:

- The Department will provide operation and maintenance services for supply of water to new developments located in unclaimed service areas
- Financial responsibility for constructing such water systems or extensions will rest with the developer
- Construction will take place by private contractor in accordance with the CWSP Minimum Design Standards
- Water supply permits, authorizations, and verifications shall be the responsibility of the developer
- Ownership of the system is to transfer to the County upon satisfactory completion of construction.

For a variety of reasons, satellite service by the County was not implemented. (Vol. 6, A-17, pp. IV 1-2) Instead, the 1994 CWSP Update names the City of Walla Walla as the satellite service agency, and provides:

> The SMA program shall require annexation of developments to the City as a condition of water service, only for developments located within the Walla Walla/College Place urban growth area, as established pursuant to the Growth Management Act. For areas inside the planning area, but outside the urban growth area, the City will own and operate the system, but annexation will not be a requirement. (Vol. 16, A-17, p.VII-4)

The plan also recommends "that the City of Walla Walla, or an alternative, single Regional Wholesale Supply System be pursued," and details the benefits to the region, including:

- The ability to manage all groundwater withdrawals to reduce localized declines;

- The optimization from cost water quality perspective, of the conjunctive use of the surface or groundwater supply

- The designated urban growth area will have urban level water service and fire protection regardless of the current designation of service area; significant reduction in water quality sampling costs for all Group A systems

- Reduction in reliance on a pumped pressure system for some utilities by making available the benefits of the City of Walla Walla storage facilities;

- Reduction or elimination of the need for certified operators by relying on the City of Walla Walla to meet this regulatory requirement; reduce or eliminate the requirement for a separate Water System Plan by deferring the planning to the City of Walla Walla, and

- Development of a stronger and more coordinated approach in representing the public water supply needs of this urban area in water rights issues.

An additional reason to avoid a multiplication of small systems is their diminished capacity to provide an effective conservation program needed for proper stewardship of limited water supplies, estimated to be only half that of larger systems. (Vol. 6, A-17, pp. VIII-3-11)

The plan also emphasizes the increasing demands on the declining basalt aquifer and the resulting importance of developing a regional water supply system utilizing both surface and ground water.

As shown in the current Walla Walla/College Place Wellhead Protection Study, groundwater levels within the basalt aquifer are significantly declining. The following water supply plan outlines the strategy for providing adequate, safe water supply to the urbanizing area (the CWSSA) of Walla Walla County given this decline….

- *Development of a Regional Supply System* based on a conjunctive use of surface and groundwater sources of supply to reduce the withdrawal from the basalt aquifer during periods of high flows in the surface water…
- *Development of Wholesale Water Agreements* between the City of Walla Walla, as the Regional Water Supplier, and the individual water utilities throughout the urban area…

Conjunctive use is a potential benefit for all of the groundwater supply systems in the urban area. Implementation of the Regional Supply System…will provide the basis to begin to manage the surface and groundwater resources of the Walla Walla basin to the benefit of all systems and users within the area…

The WUCC has determined through this CWSP update that the supply strategy adopted in the 1984 Plan is still valid. Full implementation of the 1984 strategy will result in a regional supply system that provides for the conjunctive use of the area's surface and groundwater resources and combined regional storage facilities. (Vol. 6, A-17, pp. X-1-2, 5, 18)

The proposed wholesaling for this project by the Port of Walla Walla exclusively from groundwater to supply a new water system to be established by respondent Pennbrook within the UGA is contrary to multiple, significant policies of the Walla Walla/College Place Coordinated Water System Plan. Because of their significance, an environmental impact statement should be required to provide Walla Walla County with sufficient information on the environmental consequences of not implementing these policies for this project, and to otherwise accomplish the general protection purposes of SEPA under RCW 43.21C.030(2)(c).

Conclusion 1.F.2 that the use of Port water would not conflict with adopted County policies is an erroneous interpretation of the law and a clearly erroneous application of the law to the facts under RCW 36.70C.103(1)(b) and (d).

### 3. The Proposed Project Contravenes the Walla Walla Watershed Plan

A key element in the management strategies for local water resources is the recharge of the deep aquifer by the City of Walla Walla under an Aquifer Storage and Recovery Program (ASR). The importance of this program is described in the May 2005 Walla Walla Watershed Plan (WWWP) prepared under Chapter 90.82 RCW, the Watershed Management Act, by the WRIA 32 Planning Unit with the assistance of a wide range of stakeholders led by Walla Walla County and its Watershed Planning Department,. (Vol. 6, A-18, Participants), as follows:

> **7.3.2 Recharge Enhancement**
> …(G)roundwater use has increased significantly over the past 50 to 60 years causing water level declines in the basalt aquifer around the City of Walla Walla. The declining water levels threaten the long-term viability of pumping these aquifers….
>
> *Aquifer Storage and Recovery*
> By enhancing recharge to the deeper basalt aquifer, the rate of water level declines in the aquifer can be reduced, or even reversed. In areas where water availability is limited on a seasonal basis, excess (surface) water can be injected or infiltrated into groundwater aquifers during wet periods and then withdrawn during dry periods to aid in meeting water demands. This process, known as Aquifer Storage and Recovery (ASR), serves to optimize the use of existing water supplies, especially in areas dependent primarily upon surface water supplies. The City of Walla Walla is including ASR as a key component of its long-term water supply plan...
>
> The City of Walla Walla should continue to develop ASR as a means to recharge the basalt aquifer and meet seasonal peak demands. (Vol. 6, A-18, pp.7-7,8; see also Objective BW10 at ES-3, and 3-16, 17.)

The Walla Walla Watershed Plan also addresses the need for regional coordination utilizing conjunctive use through existing rather than new suppliers:

### 7.3.4 Regional Coordination…

The specific Planning Unit recommendations with respect to regional coordination are as follows:

- Update Walla Walla/College Place Coordinated Water System plan to identify actions, strategies, roles and responsibilities for improving surface and groundwater monitoring, management and conservation, conjunctive use strategies and updating regional coordination efforts. The focus of regional coordination should be on developing a well-managed supply-diversion program, which relies on conjunctive use of the Mill Creek source and existing basalt aquifer wells.

- New urban or suburban developments or industrial facilities that require new or expanded water supplies should seek water from existing municipal or other water suppliers rather than developing separate sources of supply…

- Public water supplies should be developed from the basalt aquifer and pumping wells should be located in areas that are not currently experiencing significant water level declines. (Vol. 6, A-18, pp.7-9)

Before approving a development application that would violate the policies of the Walla Walla Watershed Plan adopted by Walla Walla County and other local governments, an EIS should be prepared, fully analyzing the adverse environmental impacts of such violations and any available alternatives.

### 4. The Cumulative Effects of the Violation of Multiple State and Local Water Policies Demonstrates a Significant Adverse Impact on the Environment

In addition to demonstrating significant impacts through conflicts with specific state and local laws and requirements for the protection of the environment under WAC 197-11-330(3)(e), WAC 197-11-330(3)(c) provides for a showing of significance when several impacts that may each be marginal are considered together.

The proposal for wholesale water to be supplied by the Port of Walla Walla wholly from groundwater to a new water supply system to be administered privately by the applicant, from wells in hydrologic continuity with the City's aquifer recharge program, is contrary to each of the following state and local policies which together demonstrate a significant, adverse impact on the environment for which an environmental impact statement should be required:

1. RCW 90.54.10(2) encouraging water supply systems that serve the general public and discouraging water supply systems that do not serve the general public,

2. RCW 70.116.040(1) prohibiting new public water systems within a Critical Water Supply System boundary area where an existing water purveyor is able to provide water service,

3. Walla Walla-College Place Coordinated Water System Plan provisions designating the City of Walla Walla as the water supplier for new development within the Urban Growth Area,

4. Walla Walla-College Place Coordinated Water System Plan provisions designating the City of Walla Walla as the exclusive Satellite System Agency with responsibility to provide water service to new developments located within portions of the Critical Water Supply System Area not designated as the service area of existing utilities,

5. Walla Walla-College Place Coordinated Water System Plan recommendations regarding the benefits of the City of Walla Walla, or an alternative agency, serving as a single Wholesale Supply System for the region, rather than having multiple wholesalers of water supplies.

6. Walla Walla-College Place Coordinated Water System Plan and Walla Walla Watershed Plan provisions for development of a Regional Supply System based on a conjunctive use of surface and groundwater sources of supply to reduce the withdrawal from the basalt aquifer during periods of high flows in the surface water.

7. Walla Walla Watershed Plan recommendations that new urban or suburban developments or industrial facilities that require new or expanded water supplies should seek water from existing municipal or other water suppliers rather than developing separate sources of supply.

8. Walla Walla Watershed Plan provisions regarding the importance of continuing and protecting the City of Walla Walla's Aquifer Storage and Recovery Program.

The Hearing Examiner's conclusion (see I.F.2, and I.F.6) that the appellant has not met its burden of proof with respect to conflicts with local and state water laws or requirements is an erroneous interpretation of the law and a clearly erroneous application of the law to the facts under RCW 36.70C.103(1)(b) and (d).

**5. No Sufficient Analysis Has Been Made Of Groundwater Impacts And Water Supply Alternatives**

Despite the failure of the respondent's environmental checklist to address in any way the groundwater and utility issues presented by the project, analysis has since been directed at the relationship between the Port of Walla Walla's wells and the City of Walla Walla's municipal water supplies, both by the applicant's expert and appellant's experts. All of these analyses acknowledge the lack of a complete understanding of the proposal's impacts on public water supplies for the Walla Walla area, including the effects of increased pumping on the affected Block 1 of the basalt aquifer shared by the Port and City wells, and the extent of the vulnerability of surface water from the Mill Creek watershed. The applicant's expert, Mr. Tim Flynn, admitted he had done no testing, nor has anyone else, to determine the water budget (inflow and outflow) within Block 1 of the aquifer which the Port shares with the City's principal withdrawal and recharge Well #1, as well as #2 and #3 to determine the effects of increased pumping by the Port for this project (Tr. 108). He also acknowledged that the amount of natural recharge, which controls availability, is uncertain (Tr. 91). At the same time, he acknowledged the importance of the City's recharge program for maintaining surface water instream flows and for providing municipal water supplies in the event of a catastrophic fire in the Mill Creek Watershed (Tr. 93-94).

The appellant's experts, Dr. Jon Cole of Walla Walla College and well drilling consultant Charles Pat Jungmann also emphasized the critical role the aquifer recharge program and the Block 1 aquifer play in the community's water supply. Their testimony highlighted the limits of that aquifer block, the risk and consequences of a watershed fire, and the need for more information on the potential adverse effects of additional pumping from that block by the Port to serve this project (Tr. 32-35, 42-46).

The conclusion of the applicant's expert was limited to an opinion that the Port could pump additional water for the project under its existing water certificate without impairing the legal rights of other users, based on consideration of the entire watershed basin's water budget, and very limited data regarding the affected aquifer block (Tr. 92-94). He did not claim there would be no interference with other water users, which he acknowledged is important to avoid (Tr. 92), and refused to state that there would be no adverse effects on local water supplies (Tr. 101).

In addition to a lack of sufficient analysis of the effects of groundwater pumping for this project, there has been no analysis of the effects of the project's water supply proposal on general water management planning policies and practices in the Walla Walla Basin, as detailed in the Walla Walla Watershed Plan and the Coordinated Water Supply System Plan, or on the effects on surface water of the planned drawdowns of ground water.

The results of the hydrogeologic studies that have been cited provide clear evidence of connectivity of the Port's wells with the adjacent City wells. This evidence dates back to 1960 in connection with the application for the water right for the airport well, which was protested by neighbors and the City, and continuity was formally found by the state water department (Vol. 6, A-8, note 35, UB, 2-22-06); see Attachment D. Despite this continuous evidence, as well as substantial conflicts between the proposed water supply system and state and local policies, no analysis has been undertaken of alternatives for water supply to the site, such as provision of water by the City of Walla Walla as is called for in all of the policies and plans.

The impacts from drawdowns of the deep basalt aquifer and the availability of alternative water sources cannot lawfully be disregarded under SEPA. See *Norway Hill,* supra, (requiring "actual consideration of environmental factors") and RCW 43.21C.030(2)(e) requiring consideration of alternative courses of action where conflicts exist concerning alternative uses of available resources.

Because the conflicts with adopted water policies are significant and because the drawdowns of block #1 of the deep aquifer create significant impacts to the region's water resources, an EIS should be prepared.

a. **The proposal is a specific threat to the Walla Walla area's water system.**

i. *The City's Mill Creek surface water system is highly vulnerable to fire.*

The proposed water supply for the Illahee development would exacerbate the risk to the City's water supply posed by fire, another impact that failed to receive actual consideration. WAC 197-11-444(1)(c)(v) (impacts to public water supplies require consideration in environmental review under SEPA.)

The serious vulnerability of the surface portion of the water supply system for the Walla Walla urban area is graphically described in the City of Walla Walla Comprehensive Water System Final Report, June 2006, (Vol. 6, A-30), as submitted by the City to the Department of Health, and was discussed by the expert witnesses. The City's report states:

> The Mill Creek watershed provides the City with one of the few unfiltered surface water systems in the Country. The City relies on Mill Creek for at least 87% of the source of

the City water supply each year…There are a number of challenging issues affecting the future of the City's water system:

- A wildfire could damage the watershed and cause an interruption of the water supply from Mill Creek, for worst case up to 5 years;
- Water supply from the watershed…is low during the summer;
- Bull Trout and Steelhead have been listed as threatened species in Mill Creek…
- …Expansion of the City's ASR (aquifer storage and recovery) program may be necessary to maintain the groundwater supply…(p.1-1)

This vulnerability is highlighted in the plan as follows:

> The second scenario will depart from previous approaches in evaluating peak supply by explicitly recognizing the limited supply and high vulnerability of the surface water supply during the peak demand flows. In the summer of 2003, the City was faced with exceptionally low stream flows, an exceptionally long hot dry spell, and increasing fecal counts in raw water reservoirs all within the same four weeks time. In addition, the Forest Service has warned the City that a high risk of catastrophic fire exists in the watershed. A study is currently underway to attempt to determine the impacts to the City's water supply. Until the risk can be conclusively quantified, the City will not rely on surface water supplies to meet peak demands…

> Well production and aquifer levels would be expected to drop, if groundwater pumping was relied upon to supply all demands for an extended period of time. Additionally, conservation measures would not reduce consumption sufficiently to offset additional demand from growth.

Additional analysis of these prospects appears at p. 3-31, from 4-19 to 4-22, and at 5-22, including the following:

> For planning purposes, the City assumes the basalt aquifer can supply the City in the event of a fire for up to five years. However, this assumption becomes less tenable as annual system demands increase over time. (p.4-19)

> Without additional treatment or new facilities, the City is assuming a five-year planning horizon for a complete loss of surface supplies…(p.4-21)

The increasing general evidence of climate change and global warming, of which the court can take judicial notice under ER 201, can be expected to further decrease available surface water flows, to increase the risk of major wildfires such as those that have occurred very near the watershed in the last two years, and to exacerbate water demand.

***ii. The basalt aquifer system is vulnerable to depletion if not conjunctively used.***

The applicant's water expert testified that the stabilization and recovery of the aquifer in Block 1 was not due to increased natural recharge, but to stabilized pumping beginning in the 1970's as well as artificial recharge by the City (Tr. 91). This is confirmed in Aspect's report in (Vol. 5, #6, p. 3), which states, "The water level decline in the basalt aquifer between 1950 and the mid-1960s is primarily attributable to the onset of large-scale groundwater pumping…" Even after stabilization of groundwater pumping, in 1982 a Critical Water Supply Service Area was declared by Walla Walla County, to include the project site and vicinity (Vol. 6, A-16, pp.I-2, I-3).

Increased pumping by the Port to serve this project would threaten a reversal of the current recovery, as well as neutralizing and exploiting the effects of the City's recharge program by diverting the artificially stored water from its intended use for municipal residents throughout the area. The applicant's expert also noted that the artificial recharge effort in the basalt aquifer tends to have a favorable effect on the shallow gravel aquifer as well as on surface waters through increased pressure from below (Tr. 93-94), another potential impact not analyzed by the MDNS. The favorable effect of the recharge program on surface water supplies would be lessened by any increased pumping for the project by the Port, rather than utilizing an alternative conjunctive-use supplier.

In view of the lack of study of the specific aquifer block that serves the City's primary supply and recharge wells as well as the Port's wells, and the critical importance of that aquifer for the City's future supplies, Conclusion 1.F.5 that the MDNS is based on reasonably sufficient information demonstrating the absence of probable, significant impacts is an erroneous interpretation of the law and a clearly erroneous application of the law to the facts under RCW 36.70C.103(1)(b) and (d).

**6. The Project's Water Supply is Not Exempt Under SEPA and Mitigation Should be Required**

The respondents seek to avoid SEPA review of impacts on ground water movement, quantity and quality, and public water supplies under WAC 197-11-444(1)(c)(iv-v) through exemption under WAC 197-11-800(4) relating to the appropriation of water rights. This proposal does not relate to appropriation of water, but to the new wholesaling of water by an existing supply system to a new water supply system for this project, an action not within the scope of the cited exemption. Conclusion 1.F.3 is an erroneous interpretation of the law and a clearly erroneous application of the law to the facts under RCW 36.70C.103(1)(b),(d).

Even were there an exemption, under WAC 197-11-305(3)(b) a proposal is not exempt where, as here,

> The proposal is a segment of a proposal that includes: (i) A series of actions, physically or functionally related to each other, some of which are categorically exempt and some of which are not; or (ii) A series of exempt actions that are physically or functionally related to each other, and that together may have a probable, significant adverse environmental impact in the judgment of an agency with jurisdiction...

The role of the water supply plan for the largest project of its kind in the history of the Walla Walla valley as well as its impacts are both physically and functionally related to other segments of the proposal. When taken together there is little doubt these actions may have a significant adverse impact on the local area if not adequately studied, conditioned and mitigated.

The respondents further assert that Walla Walla County has no power to require mitigation or conditions related to water, and that the Port and respondent Pennbrook can do anything they want with the Port's existing water right, despite any damage they may cause the environment and the public. That is clearly not the law. Authority over the ability to supply water to the public and to new development is clearly retained by state and local authorities through a variety of statutes, regulations, and ordinances in the context of specific development projects or water plans, as provided in provisions of the State Environmental Policy Act, the Water Resources Act of 1971, Chapter 90.54 RCW, the Public Water Systems Coordination Act, Chapter 70.116 RCW, and the State Building Code, Chapter 19.27 RCW, detailed above.

Under SEPA, the decisions and actions of the County in exercising its powers and responsibilities must be informed by environmental analysis. WAC 197-11-060(4)(b) also makes clear that the scope of environmental analysis is not limited to matters within the authority of the reviewing government, declaring, "In assessing the significance of an impact, a lead agency shall not limit its consideration of a proposal's impacts only to those aspects within its jurisdiction, including local or state boundaries."

In addition to authority under SEPA and the building code, in the case of an applicant for an Urban Planned Community under the UPC chapter of the Walla Walla County Code enacted at the respondent Pennbrook's request, the county has broad discretion to impose conditions on a development for the public welfare. Section 17.14.030 of that chapter provides in part:

> The applicant shall submit a draft development agreement under Chapter 36.70B RCW and as provided below (containing)…
>
> C. Measures to adequately address impacts to public services and facilities.
>
> D. Measures to mitigate State Environmental Policy Act significant adverse impacts.
>
> E. Development standards which may differ from those otherwise imposed under the Walla Walla County Code in order to provide flexibility to achieve public benefits and encourage modifications that provide the functional equivalent or adequately achieve the purposes of county standards. Any approved development standards that differ from those in the Walla Walla County Code shall not require any further zoning reclassification, variance from county standards or other county approval apart from that specified in the development agreement.

In combination with and independent of other provisions of law, these development regulations give the County authority to impose standards and conditions regarding water use and supply sufficient to protect the public interest, as well as the duty to inform the exercise of that authority through the SEPA process.

Appropriate mitigation under SEPA and conditions imposed under the UPC code can and should be required to adequately address adverse impacts of the project on public water systems and supplies. An obvious and appropriate mitigation and project condition would be a requirement that the project obtain its water supply from the City of Walla Walla, as provided in all of the cited water policies. Such a condition would assure an adequate water supply to the project and its residents, as well as protecting both the ground and surface water supply system for the entire Walla Walla community.

Conclusion 1.F.1 indicating the County has no authority to regulate the supply of water to this development is an erroneous interpretation of the law and a clearly erroneous application of the law to the facts under RCW 36.70C.103(1)(b) and (d).

## D.  THE APPELLANT HAS MET ITS BURDEN OF PROOF WITH RESPECT TO ENVIRONMENTAL HEALTH IMPACTS.

*Conclusion I.C.1 is not supported by substantial evidence and is an erroneous interpretation of the law and a clearly erroneous application of the law to the facts under RCW 36.70C.103(1)(b), (c) and (d).*

Environmental health, including releases or potential releases to the environment such as toxic or hazardous materials, risk of explosion, and noise, are elements of the environment which must be considered with respect to any project.  WAC 197-11-444(2)(a)(i-iii).

### 1.  The Project Involves Significant Impacts To Environmental Health Related To the Potential Release of Hazardous Materials

Although the environmental checklist prepared by the applicant makes no mention of the presence or risk of release of toxic or hazardous materials at multiple facilities immediately adjacent to the project site, this omission was repeatedly raised by City of Walla Walla staff in their comments on the project (Vol. 5, 19.04, pp. 1-2; Vol.1, #60, doc 1.b, pp.1-2, doc. 1.c, p.1). Without any substantial analysis of these risks, the MDNS analysis concludes that "No mitigations are in place today on surrounding properties and none are necessary at the project site as a significant adverse impact is not probable."  (Vol. 6, C-5, Memo, p.31)

The Walla Walla County Emergency Management Department lists two hazardous material sites, the City of Walla Walla's chlorine water treatment plant and the McGregor Company anhydrous ammonia storage facility, directly adjacent to the project site; a third, the Wilbur-Ellis anhydrous ammonia facility, is close by (Vol. 6, A-13; Vol. 1, #60, doc, 1.d).  .  The project site, currently open farmland, is immediately downwind from each of these facilities, and is within the serious injury zone for the documented worst case scenario for each site (Vol. 1, #55; Vol. 6, A-14).  According to the Emergency Management Department's HIVA (Hazard Identification and Vulnerability Assessment):

> Walla Walla County is at risk for a variety of hazardous materials incidents.  The majority of serious life-threatening hazardous materials incidents in this area are related to Anhydrous Ammonia….There is a great likelihood that an event involving one or more hazardous materials will occur in the next 25 years, so a rating of HIGH PROBABILITY is assigned….  The potential impact of a hazardous material incident depends on the nature of the material, conditions of the release, weather at the time of release, and area involved.  Releases may be small, easily handled and with negligible impact, or catastrophic, with immediate impact and long-term public health, habitability and environmental consequences (Vol. 3, #60, doc. 1.d, pp.19ff).

The potential impacts of the adjoining hazardous materials facilities on the project site were analyzed by Dr. Robert Rittenhouse, a professor of chemistry at Walla Walla College in two letters and slide presentations (Vol. 1, #57; Vol. 4, #98; Vol. 6, A-33), see Attachments E and F, and in testimony (Tr. 47-57). In his July 19, 2006 letter, Dr. Rittenhouse summarized his findings as follows:

1. Large scale storage of extremely hazardous materials and high-density housing are fundamentally incompatible neighbors. The consequences of a major containment breach could be horrific involving scores of fatalities and far more seriously injured.

2. The proposed Illahee development would position a hundred or more homes in the worst possible location immediately downwind of the WW city chlorine storage facility and the McGregor anhydrous ammonia tank. This situation would put the lives of many residents in danger and expose even more residents to the threat of serious injury to their eyes, lungs, and skin.

3. Historical weather data for Walla Walla shows that the most common weather pattern is one that would produce the most serious consequences in the event of a chemical release. Driven by a light wind, residents of the nearest homes would have less than 5 minutes to evacuate the premises or don gas masks.

4. The Hazardous Materials Study performed by the WW County Emergency Management Department reveals that a number of hazardous material release accidents have occurred in the County, including a major release of anhydrous ammonia…in 1996. Even though the probability of a major chemical release incident at either site cannot be precisely quantified, the accident history in the county and the state should convince us that the possibility of an accident is very real and, given the potentially castastrophic consequences, must be taken into account in county development planning. (Vol. 3, #57)

In his August 16, 2006 letter, Dr. Rittenhouse added,

I have recently obtained a copy of the WCS's (worst case scenarios) filed with the EPA by both Wilbur-Ellis and McGregor for the sites close to the proposed Illahee development. Two points emerge from both of these WCS's that strongly deserve your attention:

1. The "Distance to Endpoint" reported in both WCS's, i.e. the radius of the area that may be impacted at a serious level by the worst case spill (1.12 miles for McGregor and 6.00 miles for Wilbur-Ellis) includes the entire proposed Illahee development plan.

2. Apparently, (by their own report), neither facility has any monitoring/detection systems in place other than "visual". The McGregor site has no passive mitigation measures in place, e.g. dikes or berms.

Although the agricultural chemical facilities pose a significant hazard that should not be underestimated, my greatest concern pertains to the city's chlorine storage facility due to the combination of extreme toxicity and the physical properties of high molecular mass and a slow diffusion rate that creates the possibility of a cohesive lethal vapor plume being propelled through a dense residential center by a light wind…

The most effective mitigation of the chlorine hazard would be to convert its clorination process to one that uses a solid hypochlorite chemical rather than pure elemental chlorine. A solid chlorinating agent is far safer, though far more expensive…

The single point that I would like to leave you with is that there is substantial reason to be concerned about the prospect of a dense residential area positioned immediately downwind of hazardous chemical storage facilities….It would be irresponsible to proceed with the proposed development without further in depth study of the exact nature and extent of the risk, and the formulation of specific and adequate mitigation measures. (Vol. 4, #98)

In addition, the applicant's expert, Jay Witherspoon, testified that all three of the hazardous chemical facilities adjoining this site are in Program 3, the Environmental Protection Agency's highest risk category (Tr. 72).

## 2. No Sufficient Analysis Has Been Made of Environmental Health Impacts and Alternatives Relating to Hazardous Materials Affecting the Project

The applicant's expert testified regarding the major impacts an accidental release of toxic chemicals can have on the surrounding environment. He also testified that the risk of sabotage by a disgruntled employee or from terrorism are among the major risks to be analyzed, and should be included in local planning. (Tr. 80, 82) On cross-examination, he admitted he did not know whether the current Risk Management Plan (RMP) for any of the three hazardous chemical facilities immediately upwind of the project site had analyzed such risks, and acknowledged that a major release under those circumstances was possible (Tr. 82-84)

The Risk Management Plans for the two anhydrous ammonia facilities were not analyzed in the MDNS and were not made available to the hearing examiner or the appellants, though respondent Pennbrook's expert testified he was given access to them. The Haz-Operational reviews or studies for these facilities, referred to by the witness as a critical part of any risk management plan, were also not made available to the Hearing Examiner or the appellants, and it appears Mr.Witherspoon did not review them (Tr. 76, 77, 80, 82-83). The RMP for the City of Walla Walla's chlorine treatment plant was provided, Vol. 1, #57, though only after the issuance of the MDNS. It is apparent from the data on p. 6 of the City's RMP relating to major hazards considered and identified that no analysis of employee sabotage or terrorist activity was included in the plan, which should have been disclosed under "other". Mr. Witherspoon first denied this lack of analysis, then admitted he didn't know whether it such an analysis has been done or not (Tr. 82-83).

The City's RMP lists four 1-ton containers of chlorine online at any time and four more 1-ton containers in storage on the site, plus six 150# containers, which are contained "in a fully enclosed building whose doors and louvers are normally closed during operation of the process." (p.3) The "worst case scenario" described in the plan which results in a toxic endpoint of 0.8 miles covering most of the project site, assumes the storage building is fully closed. In addition, the effect of a release from only one of eight major containers was considered (p. 4-5). This would not be realistic in the case of intentional sabotage by a disgruntled employee or terrorist activity, when both the building and all containers could be opened, creating a far more serious incident than that analyzed. Further, Mr. Witherspoon testified that the goal of the RMP "is to assess all likely and unlikely release scenarios, develop a preventive program and mediation to handle that, and then communicate with the local responders." (Tr. 77) Mr. Witherspoon's testimony emphasized the degree of health impacts from the unknown rupture or intentional release of even one of the eight containers, which he described as being higher than for a plane crashing into such a facility, which is another acknowledged risk. In a plane crash, he explained, emergency responders can be dispatched to the area to evacuate people, while there may be no notice of an intentional release or opportunity to notify and evacuate people (Tr. 77). Those who may be sleeping in the vicinity, for example, or who are otherwise unaware of the threat, would have no opportunity to escape prior to the toxic plume taking effect.

The RMP for the City site assumes a population of only 63 people within the .8 mile toxic endpoint distance in all directions (p. 3). Respondent Pennbrook's proposal would intentionally place an additional 365 residences plus a hotel, restaurant, and other tourist facilities in the same zone and immediately downwind from the release site. Nonetheless, the applicant's expert concluded that there would be no increased risks to residents of the proposed project. His reasoning was that the risk of a release occurring would technically be the same whether there were 1 victim or 900 victims. Therefore, intentionally placing many more people in jeopardy as the project proposes to do would not change the RMP's for the sites (Tr. 71, 79, 81-82). This reasoning of course ignores the fact that while not increasing the risk of release, intentionally placing many people in the risk zone would greatly increase the impacts of a release.

A further failure of environmental analysis is that no attention has been given to the transportation of chemicals to any of these sites, including transportation of one-ton chlorine containers to the City site. The County Emergency Management Department's Hazardous Inventory Vulnerability Assessment identifies transportation of hazardous materials as one of the most serious risks facing the county (Vol. 3, doc 1.d). In addition, the director of the Emergency Management Department indicated that be believes the risk of an incident is much greater during transportation and handling of chlorine, as opposed to storage and use for water treatment (Vol. 6, C-1, p.5). No analysis of this aspect of the risk has been included for consideration by decision-makers in approving a site design.

The applicant's witness testified that sabotage by an employee or terrorist is a major risk, yet neither the risk nor its consequences were shown to have been considered in any analysis. Finding 76 is not supported by substantial evidence under RCW 36.70C.130(1)(c), since the witness acknowledged that a release such as that suggested by the applicant could occur as a result of a disgruntled or mentally unstable employee as well as a terrorist, which are within the risks the witness stated should be considered. The witness's letter report at Vol. 8, #77 also states indicates that water treatment plants are at a heightened risk with regard to vulnerability to terrorism or sabotage:

> WTP's and wastewater treatment plants are also required to perform a vulnerability assessment. The vulnerability assessment looks at site security and access by intruders, vandles (sic) and terrorists. Mill Creek WTP was required to complete a vulnerability assessment and to submit this assessment to EPA.

No evidence was presented that the required vulnerability assessment was prepared as required, or what the plant's vulnerability is with respect to external or internal sabotage.

Beyond analyzing and minimizing the risk of release, the applicant's witness testified that risk management plans are required to include an emergency response component, though no evidence was introduced as to the content of that component for these facilities or that the witness was familiar with it or how it dealt with the range of risks required to be considered. The witness testified that an emergency response component is required in order to deal with the inevitable failures which he acknowledged occur despite efforts to avoid them (Tr.72, 80-81).

Mr. Witherspoon's conclusion that there are "none to very limited risks" results from his position that adding hundreds of residences immediately downwind from these facilities would create no increased risk, the risk to a person walking or biking by the facilities and able to take evasive action being no different from the risk to persons asleep in their homes. This statement, and others by the witness, lacks credibility. Finding 65, that Mr. Witherspoon offered credible testimony in support of his opinion of no risk, is not supported by substantial evidence under RCW 36.70C.130(1)(c).

### 3. No Sufficient Mitigation Has Been Imposed For Environmental Health Impacts Relating To Hazardous Materials

In response to concerns by appellants and others, the following conditions were added to the UPC development agreement with respect to the chlorine risk by county staff, and were found adequate by the hearing examiner and county commissioners:

1. A 600 foot buffer (earth berm) between the sealed building containing chlorine gas and occupied buildings in Illahee.

2. Meetings between City staff and Pennbrook in 2014 to discuss emergency response issues related to 2010 census figures, current development in the area including Illahee, and the calculated receptor estimate.

3. A notice recorded on all plats acknowledging the existence nearby of the City's water treatment facility and the storage of chlorine gas at the facility.

As to the risk from anhydrous ammonia facilities, staff concluded, and the hearing examiner and county commissioners concurred that anhydrous ammonia does not present a significant risk to the site, and that no mitigation or conditions are necessary (Vol. 6, C-1, p.6).

Notifications on plat maps, meetings in the year 2014 between the developer and City staff, and addition of an earth berm of unspecified dimensions do not in any significant sense mitigate the impacts to the health of future residents of the site who will be downwind and within the toxic zone of potentially lethal and seriously damaging airborne releases of hazardous chemicals. The types of mitigation measures adopted may provide liability protection for the applicant and the City, but do very little to protect public health, or to substantially mitigate risk of serious impacts and injury. The weakness of these measures is indicative of the general willingness of public officials in this instance to waive, change, or ignore whatever current standards may impede the progress of this proposal.

An effective and reasonable mitigation of to the chlorine risk to the residents of this project would be to condition approval on the applicant providing for or contributing to the conversion of the City's chlorine facility to solid chlorine as described by Dr. Rittenhouse (Vol. 4, #98, see p.38 above). According to the staff report, this was also recommended by the County's Emergency Management Director, who indicated that, "although the risk was low, some risk does exist and efforts to mitigate the risk should continue. Such efforts as converting to alternative treatment processes using safer products should be explored" (Vol. 6, C-1, p.5).

Additional mitigation and possible alternatives to diminish the potential impacts to residents from the anhydrous ammonia facilities described by Dr. Rittenhouse should be explored in an environmental impact statement, including changes to the project's site plan to avoid placing housing in the most lethal zones downwind of these facilities, areas which could be devoted to recreational or agricultural uses instead (WWC Ex. 10, 78). In issuing the MDNS, no consideration was been given to these or other alternatives to deal with the identified impacts.

In addition to further environmental review and mitigation under SEPA, such conditions could be imposed under the provisions of the Urban Planned Communities (UPC) sections of the Walla Walla County Code, particularly Section 17.14.030 quoted above, which provides broad discretion to impose conditions for the public welfare, including "measures to adequately address potential land use conflicts between the urban planned community site and adjacent land uses."

It is apparent that the potential adverse impacts from each of these facilities on the population to be introduced to the project site has not been adequately analyzed, that the potential adverse impacts are significant, and that sufficient mitigation has not been adopted to justify a conclusion in the MDS that the risks disclosed are below the level of significance. Under WAC 197-11-794(2), "An impact may be significant if its chance of occurrence is not great, but the resulting environmental impact would be severe if it occurred."

Conclusion I.C.1 that these risks are remote and speculative, that those which aren't have been adequately mitigated, and that appellant has not met its burden of proof with respect to environmental health is not supported by substantial evidence and is an erroneous interpretation of the law and a clearly erroneous application of the law to the facts under RCW 36.70C.103(1)(b), (c) and (d).

The threshold determination should be overturned, and an environmental impact statement should be required in order to fully consider impacts to public health, including alternatives, prior to decision-making on the project.

## E. THE APPELLANT HAS MET ITS BURDEN OF PROOF WITH RESPECT TO HOUSING IMPACTS

*Conclusion 1.D.1 is not supported by substantial evidence and is an erroneous interpretation of the law and a clearly erroneous application of the law to the facts under RCW 36.70C.103(1)(b), (c) and (d).*

The built environment, including housing and the relationship to existing land use plans and to estimated population, is an element of the environment which must be considered with respect to any project. WAC 197-11-444(2)(b)(i-ii).

### 1. The MDNS Includes No Analysis of the Housing Impacts of the Project

No analysis has been undertaken of the impact of the proposal on local housing needs, particularly housing affordability for low and moderate income residents and workers, and the provisions of the housing element of the Urban Area Comprehensive Plan.

The primary justification for the 2005 action by the County to take this highly valued farmland into the Urban Growth Area was the established need to add to the buildable lands inventory in order to accommodate projected population growth in the Walla Walla area over the next 20 years (Vol. 8, P-10, Ordinance 322, p.10).

In the housing section of the environmental checklist, as to high, middle, and low-income housing to be provided, the applicant stated that the project will provide a range of income types, and that there will be no significant housing impacts from the proposal. In fact, no low or moderate income housing will be provided, and much of the housing proposed to be provided is intended for the second home market rather than meeting local housing needs (Vol. 4, Bk.2, I, Finding 80).

The proposal is inconsistent with the Urban Area Comprehensive Plan, whose housing element, appended as Attachment G (Vol. 6, A-28), begins with an acknowledgment of the Growth Management Act goal to "encourage the availability of affordable housing to all economic segments of the population." The element includes the countywide planning policy that, "A wide range of housing types and densities shall be encouraged and promoted to meet the needs of a diverse population and to provide affordable housing options for all income levels" (Vol. 6, A-28, p. VI-1). Under the Existing Conditions and Analysis section, the plan, prepared in 1996, references and incorporates a 1993 Countywide Housing Study that "includes a community profile of population, household composition, household income, employment, and housing stock characteristics."    The plan itself identifies increasing housing costs, including the more than doubling of home prices in the previous eight years, and substantial increases in rental rates. Under Environmental Impacts, it recognizes that "Housing supply is very critical in Walla Walla County. There is a serious shortage of available housing for various income levels, in both the rental and home ownership markets." (Vol. 6, A-28, p. VI-9)

Appellant asks the court to take judicial notice under Evidence Rule 201(d) of the continuing and worsening affordable housing problem in the Walla Walla area.

The housing needs of local residents are significant, they were not analyzed and considered in the issuance of the MDNS as required by WAC 197-11-444(2)(b)(i-ii), and the MDNS should be set aside for that and other reasons discussed in this brief.

## 2. No Mitigation Has Been Imposed For Housing Impacts

Consideration should be given to including a condition for a low or moderate income housing component either on the project site, or as off-site mitigation. No consideration was given to those or other alternatives to the proposed site use and design prior to issuance of the MDNS.

In addition to mitigation under SEPA, such conditions can be imposed under the provisions of the Urban Planned Communities (UPC) sections of the Walla Walla County Code, particularly Section 17.14.030 quoted above, which provides broad discretion to impose conditions for the public welfare not otherwise contained in the County Code.

Conclusion I.D.1, indicating that SEPA compliance is not necessary unless there are existing mandatory requirements for requiring affordable housing, is an erroneous interpretation of the law. Analysis and mitigation of probable significant adverse impacts on the supply of affordable housing in the area should be required as part of an environmental impact statement for the project.

**F.  THE APPELLANT HAS MET ITS BURDEN OF PROOF WITH RESPECT TO TRANSPORTATION IMPACTS**

*Conclusions I.A.1-2 and I.B.1-2 are not supported by substantial evidence and are an erroneous interpretation of the law and a clearly erroneous application of the law to the facts under RCW 36.70C.103(1)(b), (c) and (d).*

Transportation, including transportation systems, vehicular traffic, air traffic, movement/circulation of people or goods and traffic hazards, are all elements of the environment which must be considered with respect to any project.  WAC 197-11-444(2)(c)(i-vi).

**1.  The Project is Incompatible with the Airport Layout Plan and the Airport Safety Zone**

The Port of Walla Walla's master plan, adopted prior to its arrangements to profit from water sales to this project, discourages new housing development in the vicinity of the Walla Walla Regional Airport.

The Walla Walla Regional Airport Layout Plan Update, July 2002, states at p. A-42, (Vol. 1, #60, doc. 2.d, "In recent years, a new residential development area was permitted northeast of the airport, which could cause potential land use conflicts in the future.  Additional residential development located in the vicinity of the airport should be discouraged."  The underlying Walla Walla Regional Airport Master Plan, 1990-2010, states at p.66: "The attention of the airport operator is most often focused on facility development and financial affairs.  Yet one of the most important aspects of airport planning is the assurance of compatible on and off airport land uses…As new residential and other noise sensitive uses are developed closer to airports, there is a continued potential for conflict."

In its initial response to respondent Pennbrook's development plans, the Port, consistent with normal standards of airport management, raised concerns about "allowing housing and other non-compatible land uses to surround the airport."  The Port also wrote of its specific concerns about placing housing in the vicinity of runway 25 and 07 which lead directly over the project site.  It raised additional concerns regarding its inability to predict future needs and use of the airport, including level of use by private, commercial, and military aircraft, citing in particular the ability of the federal government to take over the airport for military use under prior agreements  (Vol. 6, A-8, note 5).

When the Port later entered into its profit-making arrangement with respondent Pennbrook to provide water, it adopted the unusual position of welcoming housing to the vicinity of the airport. It also acquiesced in a plan to locate a high density housing component of the project within the Accident Safety Zones for two runways. These zones are provided in the WSDOT Aviation Division's Airports and Compatible Land Use document, which was specifically adopted by Walla Walla County in 2005 "as a guiding document in the planning process" on the basis of which specific mitigation was to be required later at the project stage for this proposal (Vol. 8, P-10, Ordinance 322, pp.12-13), appended as Attachment I.

The Airport Compatible Land Use Matrix set out in Appendix B of the WSDOT guidelines, see Attachment J, provides for a maximum of 1 dwelling unit per acre in rural areas of Accident Safety Zone 6 and 1 du/2.5 acres in urban areas of that zone. The development site plan as proposed is inconsistent with these guidelines providing for airport compatibility, which is an important public policy set out in RCW 36.70.547 and 36.70A.510, as well in the airport's master plan, which has itself been incorporated in its entirety in the county's Comprehensive Plan as part of Policy TR-15. (Vol. 7, P-3, B)

The applicant claimed that its 98-home complex F located on the west side of the project directly across from the airport is in the accident safety zone only for runway 07/25, a secondary runway currently used primarily for private planes, rather than in the safety zone for the airport's primary runway 02/20, which presents a more serious risk. In fact, in addition to homes in the 07/25 zone which are shown in Attachment K hereto prepared by Anderson Perry(Vol. 4, #83), all of the 98 homes in area F of the site plan along with additional project homes are in the Airport Accident Safety Zone 6 for the airport's principal commercial runway, 02/20, as shown at Vol. 4, Bk.4, #82 in Attachment I also prepared by Anderson Perry, appended here as Attachment L.

As to runway 07/25, private planes of the type utilizing this runway have the greatest accident rate of any aircraft--approximately 77%--most of which occur during landing and takeoff in the vicinity of airports, according to WSDOT's Airport Compatibility Handbook, Vol. 1, #60, doc 2.b, p.13.

The WSDOT Handbook describes the general significance of the accident zones as follows:

From the perspective of safety, there are factors that determine which areas around an airport need to be protected from incompatible land uses based upon historical data. The factors include 1) the phase of aircraft operation when accidents most often occur (approach, descent, landing, takeoff, climb and cruise), 2) the major cause of accidents and incidents, 3) the location of these accidents in relation to the proximity to an airport. Based on historical data from the National Transportation Safety Board (NTSB) the areas adjacent to airports are more susceptible to aircraft accidents. Therefore, caution must be exercised when land is zoned and construction permits are issued in areas adjacent to airports in an effort to reduce the severity of an accident, loss of life or injury, based on historical records. (pp. 12-13)

The applicant's proposal seeks to place more than 3 residential units per acre within the area identified by WSDOT as Accident Safety Zone 6 for both runways, a zone designed to protect potential residents from historical risks found in locating more than 2.5 units per acre within it. (Ibid, p. 43)

In the MDNS, the only mitigation adopted is to limit land uses to those specified in an avigation easement negotiated between the Port and Pennbrook, prohibiting large numbers of people in a single location within the accident zones, protecting the airport's right to overfly and providing notification to residents of the airport's rights of operation. The provisions of this easement and particularly the attached notice to prospective residents, appended here as Attachment L-1 (Vol. 4, #82, Attachment D & E), are illustrative of the lack of protection for residents, and the focus solely on legal protection for the airport. At the same time, they provide verification of the risks the appellants have raised, acknowledging the conflicts between airports and housing, the history of continuous overflights of this property, the location of the property in airport accident safety zones, some of the impacts on residents, the possible resumption of military operations and expansion of the types of aircraft using the airport and its runways, and conflicts with industrial chemicals..

Both the environmental checklist and the MDNS are completely silent as to any analysis of the risk to residents of the project from locating housing concentrations in these zones. This documented risk to residents of homes was neither analyzed nor mitigated in the threshold determination.

Conclusion I.A.1, that rigid enforcement of the Airport & Compatible Land Use guidelines is not warranted in this case, is not supported by substantial evidence and is an erroneous application of the law to the facts. In view of the Port's Airport Layout Plan, its profit motive, and its prior inconsistent statements, its support for the proposal is not credible evidence of its safety to residents. The conclusion further fails to consider evidence of future changes in use of the airport as provided by the Port.

Conclusion I.A.2, that the 2005 rezone adequately analyzed the impacts of the project, is unsupported by substantial evidence under RCW 36.70C.130(1)(c), in that no site plan had been filed at that time, and an approval of general zoning density does not constitute approval or analysis of the impacts of a specific site plan placing residences within accident zones or future fight paths. In addition, the county specifically deferred further mitigation until the project approval stage.

The MDNS fails to mitigate a demonstrated impact to resident safety. An EIS should be required in order to fully analyze the risks from the current project plan and available alternatives.

## 2. The Project will have Significant, Unmitigated impacts on Ground Transportation

The ground traffic analysis for the project failed to consider the impacts from the nearby operation of the largest quarry in Walla Walla County, expected to generate 96 round-trip truckloads each day over Highway 12 past the project site (Vol. 4, #78, letter, p.2, UB article and ad; Vol. 6, A-12), appended as Attachment M. This activity will force additional traffic from the Illahee site onto Mill Creek Road, creating additional risk to both current users and the increased numbers of motorists, bicyclists, and pedestrians who will be using the two-lane road without shoulders because of this project. See Attachment N (Vol. 6, A-32, letter of 10-2-06).

The analysis of the appellant's transportation expert (Vol. 1, #58), concludes that the trip distribution element of the applicant's Transportation Impact Analysis "significantly underestimates the percentage of trips which would use the Mill Creek Rd./E. Isaacs Ave. Corridor..." and expresses concern

> about the safety of non-motorized users of those roads as well as the safety of motorists, given the heavy use of that route to access services by residents of the project...Even with the trip assumptions in the project's TIA, concurrency requires that Harbert Rd., Mill Creek Rd, and E. Isaacs Ave. from its intersection with Tausick Way east to Mill Creek Rd. are upgraded to safely accommodate increased motor vehicle, pedestrian, bicycle, and transit operations related to the proposed development. (p. 2)

Appellant's expert goes on to describe specific studies such as reexamination of trip distribution assumptions needed to address these impacts.

The Urban Area Comprehensive Plan states that: "Housing density and location determines level of service (LOS) demands on the transportation system....Concentration of housing in areas without adequate transportation or consideration of transportation issues results in significant adverse impacts on the total transportation system." See Attachment G, (Vol. 6, A-28, p.VI-3)

Relevant policies in the Regional and County Transportation Plans, as well as provisions of the 2005 Walla Walla Regional Bicycle and Pedestrian Plan dealing specifically with this vicinity are discussed by a member of the City's Bicycle-Pedestrian Advisory Committee at Vol. 6, A-32, along with the inadequacy of plans for Mill Creek and Harbert Road, the latter noted also by the City of Walla Walla at Vol. 1, #60, doc 1.b.

Mitigation measures needed to address impacts include upgrading Harbert Road, widening Mill Creek Rd to accommodate bicyclists and pedestrians, connections with existing bicycle and pedestrian facilities on Isaacs Avenue, and contributions to transit service which is not available to the site (Vol. 1, #58, p.3). See Attachment

Conclusion I.B.1 and I.B.2 fail to consider the quarry traffic and incorrectly evaluate the reasonableness and lawfulness of available and needed mitigation. They are not supported by substantial evidence, are an erroneous interpretation of the law, and a clearly erroneous application of the law to the facts under RCW 36.70C.103(1)(b),(c) and (d).

The further studies and mitigation considerations identified above should be considered in an environmental impact statement in order to fully analyze and reduce the adverse impacts of the project to vehicular and bicycle- pedestrian circulation and safety.

# E.   THE APPELLANT HAS MET ITS BURDEN OF PROOF WITH RESPECT TO UTILITIES IMPACTS.

*Conclusion 1.E.1 is not supported by substantial evidence and is an erroneous interpretation of the law and a clearly erroneous application of the law to the facts under RCW 36.70C.103(1)(b), (c) and (d).*

Public services and utilities, including water, sewer, and other utilities, are elements of the environment which must be considered.  WAC 197-11-444(2)(d)(vii-ix).

No utilities currently serve the site, yet no information is given in the environmental checklist, and no analysis of impacts or alternatives has been done with respect to water, sewer, gas, and electrical utilities, including construction of a major new water system by the Port.

In addition, the proposal calls for a new project water system to be owned and operated by the applicant. As detailed in the CWSP Update (Vol. 6, A-17, pp. VIII-3-11, proliferation of new water systems results in degraded conservation programs, decreased technical capacity, and less efficiency, as well as increased complexity and coordination demands for the area-wide supply system. The difficulty of increasing complexity was noted in the testimony of Dr. Cole (Tr. 33, 35). An example of existing coordination problems is presented in the City's Final Report (Vol. 6, A-30, p. 2-17). Local water plans seek to consolidate smaller area water systems under operation by the City of Walla Walla as the satellite management agency, rather than the creation and proliferation of additional small systems. (Ibid, p.1-19). The Coordinated Water System Plan expressly states, "The goal of this process is to minimize the creation of new public water systems." (Vol. 6, A-17, p. VIII-1; See also RCW 90.54.020(8)]

The record establishes the adverse impacts of the proposal on regional water utility system management. Conclusion 1.E.1 is clearly erroneous under RCW 36.70C.130(1)(b and d). Unless the proposal is mitigated by a requirement that water be supplied by the designated satellite management agency, an environmental impact statement should be required to fully analyze impacts and alternatives.

## V. CONCLUSION

As stated above, in determining whether impacts are significant, consideration must be given to the absolute quantitative effects of a proposal under WAC 197-11-330 (3)(b), as well as to marginal impacts that, when considered together, may result in a significant adverse impact, WAC 197-11-330 (3)(c). Significance can also result from conflicts with state and local laws and requirements for the protection of the environment, WAC 197-11-330 (3)(e)(iii), or from a proposal that may establish a precedent for future actions with significant effects, involves unique or unknown risks to the environment, or affects public health or safety, WAC 197-11-330 (3)(e)(-iv).

In quantitative terms, this project is the largest development Walla Walla has ever seen. The proposal for water supply solely from groundwater through a new privately operated supply system plainly conflicts with state and local water policies for the protection of the environment. In addition, the impacts of the proposal on water, water utility systems, environmental health, lands for community housing, and transportation safety, are both individually significant and, when considered together, clearly will result in a significant, adverse impact if not appropriately mitigated.

Failure to require an environmental impact statement for a project of this magnitude would establish a damaging precedent for future actions with potentially significant effects on the local environment, public health, and safety. If this project is not deemed to have significant impacts, when would such a determination ever be made in Walla Walla County?

A full environmental impact statement must be prepared in order to address this significant combination of community impacts. Alternatively, substantial mitigation should be required, or the matter remanded to the hearing officer under RCW 36.70C.130(1)(a) and (e) for further proceedings consistent with the county code and rules of procedure. In any event, the UPC permit for the development should be invalidated pending further proceedings.

Dated: March 25, 2007

Daniel N. Clark
Attorney for Appellant Walla Walla 2020
WSBA #9675

# ABOUT THE AUTHOR

Daniel Clark was born and raised in Walla Walla, Washington, where he retired from law practice in 2010. He has also written several other books, including "A Privileged Life—Memoirs of an Activist," 2013, and "Historic Sites and Markers of Walla Walla County," 2019. He can be contacted by writing to P.O. Box 1222, Walla Walla, Washington, 99362, USA, or to clarkdn@charter.net.

051019

Made in the USA
Las Vegas, NV
23 September 2021